SCIENTIFIC UNCERTAINTY, AND INFORMATION

Scientific Uncertainty, and Information

By

LEON BRILLOUIN

ADJUNCT PROFESSOR
COLUMBIA UNIVERSITY
NEW YORK, NEW YORK

1964

ACADEMIC PRESS New York and London

ACADEMIC PRESS INC.
111 Fifth Avenue, New York, N.Y. 10003 U.S.A.

United Kingdom Edition published by
ACADEMIC PRESS INC. (LONDON) LTD.
Berkeley Square House, Berkeley Square, London W.1

LIBRARY OF CONGRESS CATALOG CARD NUMBER: 64-19689

PRINTED IN THE UNITED STATES OF AMERICA

TO STEFA:

An artist's inspiration, or
a scientist's theory, reveal
the unpredictable power of
human imagination.

INTRODUCTION

Every day we read: This result is proven by science.... Our drug was scientifically tested.... Science teaches that.... The word "science" seems to contain some magic power; if put forward, it should bring immediate consent, with no possible discussion. This situation is exploited for advertisement, but it is basically unsound. Science is not a creed. It was not revealed to man by some superior deity. Science is a product of the human brain, and as such, it is always open to discussion and possible revision. There is no absolute truth in it; rather relativity is its rule. It represents a logical summary of human knowledge, based on human observation and experience, both of which are always of limited range and finite accuracy. As for the logic introduced into the classification of empirical facts, it is typically a product of our brain. We select experimental results that appear to us as logically connected together, and we ignore many facts that do not fit into our "logic." This rather artificial procedure is our own invention and we are so proud of it that we insist its results should be considered as "laws of nature."

We also select a few laws as of superior importance and we call them "principles." There are no sacred principles in science: laws are only summaries of experimental facts, selected and classified by human thinking.

Human beings are incredibly conceited fellows, too prompt to admire their own work, and to indulge in wishful thinking! Scientific theories introduce connections between empirical facts, but a *theory* may be discarded, while *facts* remain, if they have been correctly observed, and the connections will be maintained in a different theory.

Our grandsons will soon deride our simplicity, and make fun of our theories, just as we now deride the "light-ether" of old optical theories: "We now know that there is no ether, it was scientifically proved by Einstein. . . ." Let us candidly admit that we know nothing with certainty, that all our theories are open to discussion and revision and will be modified over and over again. As for the theory of light, it would be wonderful if we actually had *one* that really could be trusted. But we have to be satisfied with a strange structure, a mixture of electromagnetic fields, quantization, and relativity. When we speak of photons and of electromagnetic waves, it is obvious that unity has not yet been achieved in this field, despite many remarkable achievements. Quantum electromagnetism is still meeting strange difficulties that were recently brushed aside, but not eliminated.

In the present book, we intend to discuss the validity of theories developed in experimental sciences: in physics, chemistry, or biology. We leave out of our consideration all the possible chapters on pure mathematics, since they represent completely different problems, quite apart from the structure of the other sciences.

Science is not a mere accumulation of empirical results. It is essentially an attempt at understanding and ordering these results. What scientists are trying to do is to discover some logical frame of thinking that may enable them to find interconnections and relations between experimental observations that may be stated as "scientific laws."

The exact value and significance of these laws must be considered and weighed very carefully. They may easily be underestimated, or, on the contrary, largely overrated. Very divergent opinions have been uttered, ranging from total skepticism to blind faith in the absolute power of science. This is where a delicate and open-minded examination of the situation is actually needed. The scientist and the layman should both agree and discover together how much reliance they may have in science and how far it can reach.

Scientists always work against a background of philosophy, and while many of them may be unaware of it, it actually commands their whole attitude in research. The need for a clarification of this philosophical attitude has been deeply felt by many thinkers who spent much of their time in discussing the basic fundamentals of science. Max Planck devoted many years, in his old age, to these discussions, and his papers and pamphlets are of the highest importance. A great mathematician H. Poincaré, who was also a very remarkable theoretician in physics, wrote a few booklets that remain as great documents of scientific thinking. A. Einstein underlined some other aspects of the questions involved, and found himself in sharp opposition to views developed by N. Bohr. In this country, the great experimenter P. W. Bridgman wrote some fundamental remarks leading to his "operational method." More recently, we saw a revival of age-long discussions of "determinism *versus* probability," with L. de Broglie, and even Schrödinger, on one side, while M. Born, Heisenberg, and most theoretical physicists stood in the opposite camp.

The philosophical background of science is a very serious problem, still worth discussing, and most important for a better understanding of science. We do not expect to solve the question. It goes back to ancient Greek thinkers and it will stay open as long as scientific research itself remains alive. But even if we cannot give a final answer, we must not ignore the problem, and we shall try to explain where the difficulties lie and how they can be properly stated.

Information theory happens to be a powerful means of investigation and, in our opinion, a very safe guide—a sort of Ariadne's thread, to keep us from getting lost in this labyrinth.

The purpose of this book is not to give a definite and final answer but to look at all sides of the problem, to discuss the different possible attitudes of a thinker, and to state, as correctly as we can, the questions involved in the philosophical background of science.

This is not supposed to represent a creed for scientists to follow, but to open a discussion that may develop together with science itself, and always leave a possibility for adaptation to new situations. In a word, it is an essay, not a textbook, and we think it would be unfair to the reader to present it otherwise.

Many metaphysical creeds have been proposed, including the so-called dialectic materialism. All these artificial structures were soon discovered to be jails for free thinking.

It would have been easy enough to organize our discussion in a strictly logical fashion, and to make it look like a solid building. But this would have been entirely artificial: just as much of an artifice as the presentation of a standard mathematical textbook, with its propositions, lemmas, theorems, etc. Mathematics is not being discovered this way. It is invented piecemeal, at random; the mathematician follows his inspiration like an artist. He is actually a poet. Later on, the teacher in him takes over and writes theorems and lemmas, and the fun of discovery is gone forever.

So, we tried to avoid any prefabricated structure, for that would be a hindrance; and we did not superimpose any post-fabricated system of frames and subdivisions, for that would be false pretense. Our aim is simple, and can be explained in one phrase: unbiased free discussion.

This means unorthodox thinking, really free investigation, trying to open ways and alleys for further thinking in poorly known territory.

This means also unfinished business: all these problems, just as science itself, will never be finished. Complete achievement would mean the death of any research.

As a conclusion, we might summarize the whole discussion in a few words: the greatness and the shortcomings of theories.

The present book is divided into two parts. In the first part we discuss general problems of scientific research, especially the roles of observation, information, and imagination in the formulation of scientific laws.

The second part is devoted to classical mechanics, supposed to represent the stronghold of strict determinism. We show that this doctrine contains many uncertainties and we scrutinize the role of the great Poincaré theorem.

It was not found necessary to repeat many mathematical or theoretical proofs that could be found in other books. The reader will not be surprised to find many references to "Science and Information Theory" (1962) and "Tensors in Mechanics and Elasticity" (1961), both books by the present author and published by Academic Press.

MARCH, 1964   LEON BRILLOUIN

TABLE OF CONTENTS

PART I - INFORMATION
AND IMAGINATION IN SCIENCE

Chapter I - Thermodynamics, Statistics, and
Information 3

Chapter II - The Importance of Scientific Laws 16

Chapter III - Mathematical Theorems and
Physical Theories 32

PART II - UNCERTAINTY IN CLASSICAL MECHANICS

Chapter VIII - Weaknesses and Limitations of Mechanics 85

Chapter IX - Poincaré and the Shortcomings of the Hamilton-Jacobi Method for Classical or Quantized Mechanics 106

Chapter X - Examples of Uncertainty in Classical Mechanics 128

Part I

Information and Imagination in Science

Chapter I

THERMODYNAMICS, STATISTICS, AND INFORMATION[1]

1. SADI CARNOT—A PIONEER

Once, long, long ago, there was a lone scientist who deeply wondered about the mechanical power of steam engines; he kept dreaming and thinking about this strange phenomenon and finally published a short pamphlet about his findings. His name, Sadi Carnot[2]; the book, "Réflexions sur la puissance motrice du feu" (Paris, 1824). Carnot was 28 years old at that time and he had just discovered the famous principle that still bears his name. But he had

---

[1] Revised from articles first published in *Cahiers Pléiade* **13**, 147 (1952) (in French); *Am. J. Phys.* **29**, No. 5, 318–328 (1961).

[2] The Carnots are a famous family of scientists and political thinkers in the history of the three French Republics. The founder, General Lazare Carnot (1753–1823), was the Minister of War for the first French Republic and for Emperor Napoleon I. He won the title of "Organizer of Victory." He also was a brilliant mathematician, and his work is quoted by Sommerfeld (1952). Lazare's oldest son, Sadi Carnot (1796–1832), was the inventor of thermodynamics. His later work on the first principle is briefly quoted by Sommerfeld (1956, p. 22, footnote and p. 26) who writes: ". . . we shall follow the classical path initiated by Sadi Carnot in 1824 and then followed by R. Clausius from 1850 and by W. Thomson from 1851 onward."

Lord Kelvin repeatedly tried to discover the notebook of Sadi Carnot (25 years later!), of which he had heard through some French friends, but he could not find it.

The second son of Lazare was Hippolyte Carnot (1801–1888), Minister of Education in 1848 (second Republic) and a well-known sociologist. Marie-François Sadi Carnot (1837–1894), a son of Hippolyte, became President of the third French Republic in 1887 and was assassinated by an Italian anarchist.

The papers of Sadi Carnot, the scientist, were published by the French Academy of Sciences in 1927 under the title: "Biographie et Manuscrits de Sadi Carnot." The biography, written by the great mathematician E. Picard, is full of valuable information.

been careless enough to invent the principle we call "second" before stating the first one! And professors told him time after time, for more than a century, how wrong he had been! Professors were also wrong not to read the second book of Carnot.[2] To their credit, let us say that the second book was published only in 1927, more than a century later; and this requires a few words of explanation.

After writing his first book, Carnot kept thinking and wondering; he made short notes in a small notebook, intending to rewrite the whole thing more carefully later on. But there was no "later"; Sadi Carnot died in 1832 during an epidemic of cholera that ravaged Paris. He was then 36 and had left in his notes the detailed statement of the first principle, plus a computation of the mechanical equivalent of heat (which was only 15% off), plus a sketch of the kinetic theory and of thermal agitation! It took scientists half a century to rediscover all these fundamental ideas.

And what about the notebook? It was given to Sadi's brother Hippolyte, a sociologist, who kept the book in his library but did not suspect its extraordinary importance. Hippolyte gave this book to the French Academy of Sciences around 1878 and some abstracts of it were published at that time. Complete publication with a photocopy of the notebook occurred only in 1927. It does not seem to have attracted great attention; however, it does contain some striking statements, if you remember the date, 1830:

> Heat may be a vibrational motion of molecules. If this be the case, a quantity of heat is but the mechanical energy used up to put the molecules into vibration. . . . Heat is a motion. . . . *Total energy* [in Carnot's words, *puissance motrice*] *exists in nature in constant total amount*. It is never created nor destroyed; it simply takes another aspect. . . . Production of one unit of mechanical energy requires the destruction of 2.7 units of heat.

The computation was based on gas diffusion experiments, and was very similar to a later computation made by R. J. Mayer in 1842.

Some of Carnot's notes are not so easy to read. He had to create his own vocabulary, which we often do not understand clearly. Unquestionably, he was a pioneer. He found his way through an unknown territory and traced his own footpath, but he did not have time to build a highway for students to follow. For instance, the word "caloric" is often obscure. It used to mean "quantity of heat," but in the Carnot pamphlet, it can be best translated by "entropy," as was first noted by Bronsted and La Mer (see La Mer, 1949).

Carnot was one of the great geniuses in science, but death carried him away leaving his work tragically unfinished.

2. TWO PRINCIPLES OF THERMODYNAMICS

First Principle: Conservation of Energy

Despite its various aspects and its perpetual transformations, energy keeps an unchanged total value as long as we consider a closed system isolated from its environment. A charged battery and a weight raised to a certain height represent typical forms of energy, and may be changed into chemical energy, work, or heat. The reverse transformations, from heat into work, for instance, are also possible, with certain limitations related to the second principle.

To the usual forms of energy, Einstein added a new one: mass. Any mass possesses energy; any energy represents a given mass. The old principle of conservation of the mass is thus enlarged and integrated into the energy conservation principle.

Second Principle: Carnot

Caloric energy requires a special treatment with a sort of two-way accounting. Let us consider a machine or a physical system in contact with heat sources. We first establish an energy balance sheet of the operations, with credit and debit columns, depending on whether the machine absorbs or yields heat.

Then we use an exchange coefficient, which varies according to the temperature at which each heat transfer occurs. In dividing the quantity of heat Δq (positive or negative) by this exchange coefficient, we calculate the amount of entropy ΔS supplied, for which we keep a separate account. The exchange coefficient is none other than absolute temperature T. In the centigrade scale, it is the usual temperature, increased by 273.15°. Absolute zero corresponds to $-273.15°$ centigrade. According to this procedure, we start from a fundamental relation between the quantity of heat Δq received by a system, in the course of a given operation, and the increase of entropy ΔS in this same system.

$$\Delta S = \Delta q / T \quad \text{or} \quad \Delta q = T \Delta S \tag{I.1}$$

and we must keep an account of the quantities q and S separately.

Think of a goldsmith dealing in precious metals. He keeps an account of the weights of metal bought or sold. In another column he records prices paid or received. For each transaction mentioned in the first account, there corresponds a mention in the second column. Imagine that Δq represents the weight of metal bought, silver, for instance. If T is a weight of silver worth a dollar, ΔS is the amount of the operation in dollars. The comparison links the idea of entropy to the notion of value. We shall have further opportunity to discuss this analogy (Section 4).

Between heat and entropy, we have an exchange office, using a variable rate of change according to the temperature: a strange sort of planned economy. Still more curious is the tendency of entropy always to increase. Dip a hot metal into a container filled with cold water. A certain quantity of heat will pass from the metal into the water. The entropy lost by the metal is calculated with a very high coefficient T_1; the entropy gained by the water contains a lower coefficient T_2; thus, the entropy lost by the metal is less than the entropy gained by the water. All in all, the metal-water system has gained entropy. Here is another experiment: Let us warm up water by means of an electric resistance connected to a battery. The battery loses electric energy but very little entropy, the water gains heat and entropy. The following general rule can be deduced: For any isolated system, the total energy remains a constant, but the total entropy has a tendency to increase. The system's entropy may, at the least, remain constant (if nothing happens, or if the transformations are reversible); it can increase in the case of irreversible transformations (as in the two given examples), but the entropy of an isolated system can never decrease.

The economy of the entropy is not only planned; it follows a one-way street.

These remarks call for a definition of the total entropy S of a system. Let us suppose that we can build a system from its component parts while using only a series of reversible transformations; the heats $q_1, q_2, \cdots$ used in each operation can be observed, and the corresponding entropies $s_1, s_2, \ldots$ calculated.

The total entropy of the system can then be defined as a sum,

$$S = s_1 + s_2 + s_3 \ldots \tag{I.2}$$

of the entropies corresponding to each of these reversible steps. If some of the transformations are irreversible (explosive chemical reaction, non-compensated heat), we can no longer estimate exactly the entropy of the final system; each step that is irreversible increases the total entropy at a rate that is hard to estimate. We thus get an incomplete result:

$$S \geqslant s_1 + s_2 + s_3 \ldots \tag{I.3}$$

The actual final entropy is necessarily larger, in case of irreversibility, than the sum of the entropies of the successive steps of the buildup.

3. THERMAL ENGINES

Carnot's principle has a very important consequence: It is impossible to transform heat into work as long as only one source of heat is used. Such an operation would mean, for this sole reserve of heat, a loss in calories; therefore, a decrease in the system's entropy. This is contrary to the absolute rule that the total entropy of an isolated system must constantly increase.

Many attempts, all fruitless, have failed to establish a perpetual motion that could yield work indefinitely. Some attempts sought to obtain a mechanical type of work without compensation, in contradiction to the first principle. Others planned to extract work from a unique source of heat (using heat taken at surrounding temperature, for instance). The total failure of all these tests confirms the two principles of thermodynamics.

A thermal machine, such as the steam engine, effectively transforms a given quantity of heat into work. This operation rests on the use of *two* sources of heat at two different temperatures: the boiler filled with boiling water represents the high-temperature source (T_1); the condenser (or the exterior atmosphere) receives the cooled vapor and constitutes the low-temperature source (T_2). The machine borrows a certain quantity of entropy ΔS from the source T_1, and this represents a certain quantity of heat

$$\Delta q_1 = T_1 \Delta S \tag{I.4}$$

according to our rule of accounting in the previous section; this heat is carried by the vapor through the cylinders. After having supplied work, in pushing the pistons, the vapor has cooled and escaped to the condenser (at temperature T_2); there it is condensed and liberates a quantity of heat

$$\Delta q_2 = T_2 \Delta S \tag{I.5}$$

Since $T_2 < T_1$, the heat obtained Δq_2 is less than the heat borrowed Δq_1. The difference $\Delta q_1 - \Delta q_2$ has been transformed into mechanical work in the cylinder of the engine. We find here, almost literally, Carnot's definition with just one slight change of "caloric" into "entropy."

This operation would correspond to an ideal machine, by which we mean "reversible." It can be exactly reversed: steam can be extracted from the cold source. A pump does the work, compresses the steam, and heats it up; then the hot steam is given back to the hot source; Δq_1, Δq_2, and the work all have signs just opposite those in the previous operation.

What is this machine? A refrigerator, no less! The motor of the refrigerator does the work necessary to extract heat from the cold container and bring it to the exterior temperature (hot source). The machine maintains a low temperature in the storage part of the refrigerator and constantly warms up the kitchen where the appliance stands.

When an operation is revresible and can be done at will in one direction or the other, the entropy remains constant. It cannot decrease in either operation. In fact, it is not quite that simple. It is inevitable that any given operation shows some characteristics of irreversibility (frictions, heat losses, etc.) which bring on a certain increase of entropy. The actual machine is never equal to the ideal machine. A perfect reversibility is not feasible, but the best machines have outputs which are only slightly inferior to those of the ideal machine.

4. Entropy and Value, Negentropy, and
Energy Degradation

Carnot's principle presents a very curious characteristic: it indicates a general tendency in the evolution of the physical world. In the course of time, entropy must constantly increase in any closed and isolated system. There is no turning back. At this point, we must embark upon a discussion, for we shall later have to take into account the modalities and possibilities of extension in order to see how the principle may be generalized, and whether it can be extended to other phenomena.

Let us first try to define what is understood by "energy degradation" in physics and in chemistry. Let us classify the different sources of energy, and give the highest mark (A) to those which are integrally transformable into all the others, and reserve the lower class (C) for heat, whose transformations are limited by Carnot's principle:

A. Mechanical work, electric energy.
B. Chemical energy.
C. Heat.

Chemical energies occupy the B position because of caloric effects that are linked to chemical reactions. The law of entropy increase results in a progressive degradation of the energies, which tend to fall from classes A and B into class C.

A clearer picture can be drawn if, according to a suggestion by Schrödinger, we introduce, instead of entropy S, an expression with an opposite sign, the negative entropy

$$N = -S \tag{I.6}$$

which we call, for short, *"negentropy."*

The entropy constantly increases in any given closed system; therefore, the negentropy always has a tendency to decrease. This negentropy represents, finally, the quality (A, B, or C) of the energy, and Carnot's principle expresses a law on loss of value, a rule on level drop. Because of ancient experience, our mind understands more easily a drop as a natural tendency; our new definition satisfies this mental habit and connects the notions of negentropy, level, and value.

In Section 2, we had started a comparison which now takes its full meaning.

A system which is capable of producing mechanical (or electrical) work will be considered as a source of negentropy; for instance, a banded spring, a raised weight, a charged battery.

Let us now consider a closed structure in which the mean temperature is T; but at a certain point there exists another temperature, T'. This is a source of negative entropy. It is immaterial whether temperature T' is lower or higher than the surrounding temperature T. In both cases, we could build a thermal engine by using the difference in temperature to produce work. We therefore have there a local reserve of negentropy. If we forget to use this possibility, the temperatures will progressively level themselves by exchange of heat among the various parts of the system: natural decrease of negentropy. The inanimate world, governed by physics and chemistry, obeys a natural law of degradation, of loss of value. This law sums up the essentials of thermodynamics, but the notion of value here remains linked to inert matter, or better, to energy. Physics has not been able to (and probably cannot) dissociate these two entities.

In other fields, it seems that "value" can be independently defined, and that it also obeys, in a great many examples, a law of natural decrease. We will try, later on, to link these two points of view more closely, and we will seek to spread the definition of negentropy far from its birth place, to expatriate it to little-known territories.

5. Entropy and Probability

Physicists have striven a long time to finally recognize, little by little, the extent of thermodynamic laws, exploring all the fields of application, and realizing the deep meaning of the two principles. These absolutely general laws apply to all fields of physics and chemistry: properties of gases, liquids, and solids; chemical reactions; electricity and magnetism; radiations; astrophysics.

For a long time, the application of thermodynamics to radiation problems remained an enigma. The mystery was cleared up only around 1900, thanks to the work of the great German physicist Planck, and it required the acceptance of revolutionary notions: quantum theory. One had to stop considering energy as a continuous phenomenon, and to admit the idea of a granular structure, an atomization whose particles have been named "quanta." This new theory met with enormous success and spread to all fields of physics and chemistry. Today, quanta and relativity form the basis of physical theories. Instead of suffering from it, thermodynamics came out of this test stronger and more lively than ever. It gives more precision to the notion of entropy and draws it nearer to the idea of probability. The chain is now made of the following links: negentropy–value–scarcity.

In the inanimate world, we confuse scarcity with value; what is exceptional is remarkable; the improbable, the unusual, is admirable. This confusion would be inadmissible in morals, in philosophy, or in criminology. Within the limits of physics and chemistry, the equivalence seems complete because we have no other criterion for quality than scarcity. In economics, scarcity represents only one factor of the price, the symbol of the value; usefulness (law of supply and demand) represents a second factor. The price of a precious metal depends on its scarcity and on the importance of the market. Physics does not know these contingencies, and omits the essential distinction.

In the whole course of the past century, neglecting the role of observation in science was a dogma, an incontestable axiom. The scientist was supposed to be satisfied by observing what went on around him. He intervened only in the planning of an experiment, and then recorded the results. His presence was not assumed to modify the events. We now are cured of these over-simplifications. Any observation (we have learned by experience) represents a perturbation, and influences the course of facts. This reaction of the observer to the observed thing seems negligible in astronomy or in classical physics, but it becomes most important when we attempt to study the remotest particles such as atoms, electrons, photons, and mesons. We are still far from having exhausted the content of these essential remarks. These ideas, new to physicists, are well known to biologists. Doctors and psychologists have long learned to beware these subtle interactions. The study of the "coupling" between the observer and the observed system, between man and physics, will probably oblige us to revise the notion of value and to dissociate it from that of scarcity, but this step has not yet been clarified.

We shall discuss these problems over and over again in the present book. The point to emphasize now is the fact that we cannot go to the extreme and measure everything in a physical system. There always remains a large number of unknown quantities about which we can state only some probabilities, but no certainty.

As a rule, entropy is directly connected with probabilities. This can be represented by a mathematical relation of the greatest importance. It was first discovered by Boltzmann, and in a different way, by J. W. Gibbs. After many comparisons and discussions, the best formula was obtained by Max Planck, who stated:

$$S_0 = k \ln P_0 \qquad k = 1.38 \times 10^{-16} \text{ C.G.S. unit} \qquad (I.7)$$

In this expression, S_0 represents the entropy of a physical system, and P_0 the number of elementary microscopic "complexions," as Planck calls them. The constant k is usually known as Boltzmann's constant, although it is not at all proven that Boltzmann actually used it; but it certainly deserves his name since he was a pioneer in that field. The numerical value given in Eq. (I.7) corresponds to C.G.S. units and centigrade degrees.

The idea of "microscopic complexions" refers to modern atomic physics, completed by quantum conditions. The general viewpoint is that a physical system may exist only in a finite number of states (quantized states); the number P_0 of these discrete states may be very large, but it can always be counted.

Let us examine the natural evolution of an isolated system. We may start from an exceptional and improbable structure, artificially built by the experimenter. Left to itself, this unstable structure will decay little by little and evolve toward more probable and more stable structures. The probability will increase; the entropy will increase. This statistical interpretation of entropy is extremely useful. But it is better than a comparison, more than a visualization. The formula lends itself to calculations; the theory lets one foresee, *a priori*, the exact value of the entropy of a system, and experimental verifications confirm these predictions.

6. THERMODYNAMICS AND INFORMATION THEORY

A new theory of information has been developed in recent years and presents many points in common with statistical thermodynamics (Seeger, 1958; Brillouin, 1959, 1962).

Let us consider a characteristic example. The gas contained in a container is composed of myriads of molecules moving ceaselessly. At a given instant of time, we have no idea of the exact positions and speeds of these particles. The microscopic structure of the system is unknown to us and we know only macroscopic, large-scale values: pressure, volume, temperature, and chemical constitution. These quantities can be measured; details of the distribution of the molecules cannot be observed.

On these bases, we compute the number of complexions of the system and its entropy. The computation takes into account all elementary internal structures satisfying our macroscopic conditions. The greater the uncertainty, the larger the number of possible internal structures, the higher the probability, and the larger the entropy.

We may sometimes possess some special information on the system under consideration; for instance, we may know how it was constituted at a given time, and hence know the original distribution of densities and velocities. The knowledge of such additional information allows us to state more accurately the structure of the system, to decrease the number of elementary complexions, and to decrease probability and entropy.

Any additional piece of information increases the negentropy of the system. This similarity leads to an important remark: we may define a quantitative measure of the information by the corresponding increase of the negentropy. Such is the conclusion of a series of discussions which have been recently published.

The additional information, obtained at a given moment, will progressively lose its value, for the system, abandoned to itself, naturally evolves toward more probable states of less negentropy. At the time of its formation, the gas had a certain distribution of densities, but the thermal agitation of the molecules stirs up the gaseous mass and rapidly produces an equalization which corresponds to a structure of less negentropy.

Such is a normal evolution. However, we may intervene. Armed with the information we possess, we can introduce walls which isolate the regions of different densities and thus maintain the structure of high negentropy and protect it against its natural destruction. The information may be transformed into permanent negentropy.

Conversely, we may also transform negentropy into information. Let us go back to the example of a gas contained in a closed vessel; we do not know anything of its internal state, but we want to learn something about it. A reasonable experimental method consists in sending a beam of light through the gas. If there are differences in densities, they will result in light scattering. By collecting the light scattered in all directions and studying its distribution, we obtain information on the distribution of the gas densities. However, such an experiment consumes negentropy! A certain amount of high-quality light energy (high negentropy) has been absorbed and transformed into heat, that is, in low-quality energy (low negentropy). Therefore, our experiment essentially consisted in transforming negentropy into information. A thorough analysis of all experimental methods of observation reveals the general character of this result: it is impossible to make any measurement in a laboratory without consuming a certain quantity of negentropy. Every type of experiment represents a transformation of negentropy into information.

The two previous examples can be coupled in a series of operations which result in the following transformations:

$$\text{Negentropy} \rightarrow \text{Information} \rightarrow \text{Negentropy}$$

The process consists in devising an experiment capable of supplying certain information and in using that information to decrease the system's entropy. The classical example of Maxwell's Demon can be brought back to a diagram of that type. Thoroughly analyzed, the problem shows that, if we start from a system with balanced densities and temperatures, the quantity of negentropy lost in the first operation is always larger than the quantity retrieved in the second step. On the whole, the transformation follows Carnot's principle. There is a degradation of energy even in its new transformations in which the notion of information is introduced. We have thus obtained the following essential results:

A. Equivalence of negentropy and information.
B. Extension of Carnot's principle to these transformations.

Let us stop and think for a moment. We give the word "information" a precise meaning, though a very restricted one indeed. We link information to negentropy, and, therefore, to improbability (Section 5).

Any notion of human value is totally excluded: moral qualities, and intellectual or artistic values are totally absent. There is actually no human element introduced in this definition and our "information" should never be confused with "science" or "knowledge." Such restrictions are very severe, but they represent the price we have to pay for a precise and objective definition of information.

7. A PRECISE DEFINITION OF "INFORMATION"

The general remarks of the preceding section lead directly to a precise, scientific definition of the word "information." This will, of course, be different from the current meaning of the word, and the reader should, from now on, keep in mind the fact that our information theory is not dealing with journalistic, or any other common kind of information, but only with the quantities mathematically defined hereinafter.

We start from the definition carefully stated at the beginning of my book "Science and Information Theory" (Brillouin, 1956, 1962, pp. 1 and 3), where it is presented in the following way:

Let us consider a situation in which P_0 different things might happen, and all these possible outcomes are supposed to have equal probability a priori. This is the initial condition, in which we have no special information about the general problem ($I_0 = 0$). But circumstances may arise in which we have some more precise definitions or measurements about a similar problem, and thus obtain a smaller number P_1 of equally probable outcomes. We state that the *information*, I_1, in this problem, can be defined by a formula

$$I_1 = K \ln (P_0/P_1) = K \ln P_0 - K \ln P_1 \tag{I.8}$$

where K is a constant, depending upon the unit system selected, and ln means the natural logarithm to the base e.

It is reasonable to use a logarithm in this formula, in order to obtain for the information an additive property. For a discussion of the general features and properties relating to this definition, the reader may refer to the book quoted above.

The value of the constant K depends only on units used in the problem. In many applications to problems of telecommunications, it has become customary to use binary digits (called "bits") and this leads to the value

$$K = 1/(\ln 2) \tag{I.9}$$

When, however, we are mainly interested in physical problems, we want to use similar units for information and entropy [Eq. (I.7)], and we take

$$K = k = 1.38 \times 10^{-16} \qquad \text{(Boltzmann's constant)} \tag{I.10}$$

This choice of units enables us to compare information directly with entropy, and we shall use it systematically in this book, where we deal almost exclusively with information or entropy related to physical systems. Let us note right away that the ratio of units (I.9) to (I.10) is very close to 10^{16}, an extremely large figure indeed. This very large number plays a prominent role in many discussions of thermodynamics, since it proves that an enormous amount of information [measured in bits, Eq. (I.9)] is needed to yield any practical contribution to entropy.

8. INFORMATION AND NEGENTROPY

Let us examine now more carefully the relation between these two quantities, and explain the exact meaning of our discussion in Section 6.

We use the definition of "entropy" according to Planck [Eq. (I.7)] and we reconsider the typical example discussed at the beginning of Section 6. We assume a physical system that might obtain a variety of distinct microscopic structures, and we call P_0 the total number of such structures, when nothing special is known about the system ($I_0 = 0$). When, however, we happen to have a certain amount of additional information I_1 on the state of our system, the number of possible structures is P_1, smaller than P_0.

Summarizing the assumptions, we state

In general

$$I_0 = 0 \qquad P_0 \text{ possibilities}$$

with some information

$$I_1 > 0 \qquad P_1 < P_0 \text{ possibilities} \tag{I.11}$$

and

$$I_1 = k \ln P_0 - k \ln P_1$$

This results directly from the definition (I.8) with units (I.10); but this formula may be rewritten when we take Eq. (I.7) into account:

General case, entropy

$$S_0 = k \ln P_0$$

Special case, entropy

$$S_1 = k \ln P_1$$

and the relation

$$I_1 = S_0 - S_1 \tag{I.12}$$

or

$$S_1 = S_0 - I_1$$

The additional information I_1 which we happen to possess about the system, in the example 1, results in a decrease of entropy. *Information* represents a *negative contribution to entropy*. This statement was presented by the author as "The negentropy *principle of information*."

It is sometimes useful to make a distinction between information relating to very general problems and information about a physical system. The latter was often called *bound information*.

REFERENCES

Brillouin, L. (1956). "Science and Information Theory," 1st ed. Academic Press, New York.

Brillouin, L. (1959). "Vie, Matière et Observation." Albin Michel, Paris.

Brillouin, L. (1962). "Science and Information Theory," 2nd ed., pp. 1, 3, 120, 152. Academic Press, New York.

Carnot, Sadi (1824). "Reflexions sur la puissance motrice du feu." Paris.

La Mer, V. (1949). *Science* **109**, 598.

Picard, E. (1927). "Biographie et Manuscrits de Sadi Carnot." French Academy of Sciences, Paris, France.

Seeger, R. J. (1958). *Am. J. Phys.* **26**, 248.

Sommerfeld, A. (1952). "Lectures on Theoretical Physics," Vol. 1: Mechanics. Academic Press, New York.

Sommerfeld, A. (1956). "Lectures on Theoretical Physics," Vol. 5: Thermodynamics and Statistical Mechanics. Academic Press, New York.

Chapter II

THE IMPORTANCE OF SCIENTIFIC
LAWS

1. The Role of Scientific Laws

The problem to be discussed now is concerned with the theoretical value of theories, or, to put it bluntly: how much information is there in a theoretical formula?

The most difficult stage in such a discussion is the discovery of how the problem can be properly stated, and how it can be connected with other problems for which a reasonable solution has already been obtained.

We start with a presentation of some remarks which this author presented in earlier papers.[1] We shall later discover a different viewpoint, and investigate the whole situation very carefully.

Here is the point of view given in 1952 *and* 1961:

In using the vague word "information," we cover a great variety of notions very different from one another. The problems discussed in Section 6 of Chapter I refer to transitory information. We know, from the way a physical system has been built, that it is in a certain unstable state; left to itself, this system evolves toward stability, which is represented by a minimum negentropy structure. The initial information loses its value little by little, while the negentropy gradually decreases.

This characteristic situation is typical of most examples in physics, and can be found again and again in many other circumstances. Meteorological information, stock market quotations, and newspaper reports represent as many passing pieces of information whose value gradually gets thinner. However, there exists another kind of information which has a permanent

---

[1] See footnote [1], Chapter I.

character: great discoveries, scientific laws. Should we mix and confuse these two types of knowledge under a single name? If a distinction is necessary, where shall we draw the dividing line?

Our original discussion continued in the following way:

The effort of thought of a scientist or a philosopher actually seems to represent a creation of new information. When Einstein formulated the principle of relativity, or when de Broglie invented wave mechanics, these thinkers really created new processes of scientific prediction. They supplied humanity with information unknown up to then. These remarks suggest the following question: Does thought create negative entropy? Reflection and the work of the brain may go in a direction contrary to that of usual physical laws; it is, however, possible that we have made too rapid an extrapolation. *The question deserves careful study.*

First of all, it seems very difficult to set a limit, to draw a border line between these two extreme categories. We could easily find many intermediate examples: empirical laws of limited extent are soon replaced by more extensive statements covering a wider field, and these open the way to the discovery of some great law of nature. These laws, as we said, are supposed to have a permanent character. Is it really true? Nothing human is really permanent. The physicists of our generation have seen Newton's mechanics replaced (or rather, generalized) by Einstein. Then wave mechanics appeared, and we are looking forward to some harmonious synthesis of the two sorts of mechanics, which complement each other without agreeing completely.

A piece of passing information, such as in the examples previously discussed, represents the result of few measurements, each of which was obtained at the expense of a certain number of negentropy units. A more general law is based on a greater number of experiments and sums up a great deal of temporary information. Its measure in negentropy is that much higher, though the balance becomes hard to establish. No limit appears in this continuity of information, only a series of more and more complex problems.

If we now consider the problems of transmission, they are very similar for all our various categories of information. A piece of information of passing value requires rapid broadcasting: this is the role of the press and the radio. A scientific law, whose extent is long lasting, spreads through scientific reviews, teaching, and books. The mechanism is identical. Speech, writing, and drafting are the transporting agents of information and thought.

However, at one essential point, new characteristics appear: reflection and thought. The information gathered from a direct experiment is, as we said, ephemeral; its negentropic measure can be established without too much trouble, for this kind of information represents only the stating of the results of a few measurements. When we arrive at scientific laws, another element is introduced: the effort of reflection. The scientific law is not only the expression of a certain quantity of empirical facts, but the thought of the scientist intervenes: selection of facts, comparisons, *imagination*, flashes of genius. We do not know very well how to analyze these new ingredients.

We could, at best, try to evaluate the number of experiments necessary to lead to the statement of a certain physical law. We could compute the quantity of negentropy consumed in these experimental measurements. It does not seem possible to compute the thought contribution, though it could correspond, as a rule, to the consumption of phosphorus in the brain! Our definitions are slipping through our fingers.

2. Scientific Laws and Negentropy

Despite these obstacles and these difficulties, we may try to keep the parallel we established and to assimilate information and negentropy. There has been a consumption of negentropy in the series of processes that led us to the discovery of a scientific law.

Inversely, the scientific law represents a method of forecasting which will enable us to build high-negentropy systems. Confident in the information contained in these laws, we invent new scientific apparatuses and we build industrial machines heretofore unknown to us. Each of these instruments represents an extremely improbable structure, which nature itself has been unable to realize. If improbability equals negentropy, then the scientific laws appear as potential sources of negentropy.

Let us expound clearly to avoid any misunderstanding. Each machine, in the course of its operation, strictly obeys the second principle. In no case will its operation contradict Carnot's principle. What we actually consider is not the output of the machine, but the process of its invention; we concentrate on the work of the engineer or the scientist who conceives a piece of apparatus and builds it. We intend to introduce here the value of the invention, the importance of the patent, and to write this in technical terms. We are attempting to take into account the creative power of thought and of its practical realization.

Can we talk of structural negentropy where a machine is concerned? The negentropy of the total structure is not the sum of the negentropies of the component parts. The entropy is no more an additive property because of the couplings of the machine's various parts. The "functional value" of these parts represents the contribution of these couplings. These very general remarks apply to all mechanisms invented by a human inventor. Take a collection of spare parts and compute their total entropy. Assemble the parts according to a blueprint and build a locomotive. Is it reasonable to assume that the entropy has not changed? The information contained in the blueprint represents a contribution to the total negentropy. And this information has been derived from the knowledge of the engineer (physical laws) and from his inventiveness (thought).

The best proof that one should consider a negentropy term as corresponding to the structural value of the machine is that there exists, in this machine, a "something" which is destroyed according to Carnot's principle. With the passing of time, the machine wears out, rusts, breaks, and stops functioning. All the processes of this gradual destruction are irreversible reactions under the jurisdiction of Carnot's principle. This "something" which is generally destroyed by Carnot's principle—what name can we give it, if not "negentropy of structure"? Functional value? This value is practically recognized in the price of the machine, it is a commercial value and it is negotiable.

3. QUANTA AND UNCERTAINTY PRINCIPLE

The preceding discussion is centered on Carnot's principle and on the possible modalities of its extension. A few words are needed to indicate the connection with modern physical theories, especially with the quantum theory. Wave mechanics gives us an excellent interpretation of the properties of atoms and molecules. It is especially successful in the explanation of chemical bonds, and the reduction of valence forces into a purely physical scheme. Thanks to the quanta, the unification of chemistry and physics is making rapid progress, and we can ascertain the considerable importance of these doctrines in the biological field. One remarkable characteristic of these theories is that they grant a greater importance to notions of statistics. Statistical thermodynamics comes out all the more vigorous and rigorous.

A new principle dominates physics now, the *uncertainty principle*, formulated by Bohr and Heisenberg. There is a limit to the accuracy of experimental measurements. The scientist seeks to increase, as far as possible, the accuracy of his observation, but he is always stopped by an unsurmountable obstacle: the perturbation brought by the measuring device itself to the object measured. In former classical theories, it was admissible to ignore the role of the observer: it was thought that the experimenter observed what was going on around him; his presence was not supposed to influence the course of events. In astronomy or in classical mechanics, this point of view is defensible. But when we examine atoms or electrons, we cannot look at these tiny elements without disturbing them. The coupling between the observer and the observed cannot be ignored any more.

Instead of basing the discussion on the uncertainty principle, one can rely upon another notion, that of *complementarity*. In fact, the two points of view are equivalent. All proofs of the uncertainty principle rest on the use of the notion of complementarity. Let us try to sum up Bohr's conceptions on the subject: electrons, protons, mesons, photons—all these essential components of the material world cannot be considered as particles in the usual sense. We must conceive them as being between particles and waves. Our customary ideas, forged after the model of everyday life, do not apply to these ultimate elements. Their nature surpasses our understanding. In certain experiments, a corpuscular description is sufficient, but in other cases, the wave representation presents itself more naturally and the quantum conditions join the two interpretations which looked contradictory at first sight.

If we use the model with particles, we have to give up describing their movements accurately. The uncertainty principle or the complementarity forces us to stop.

Absolute determinism does not apply any more. Physical laws take on an essentially statistical value, but do not apply to the detail of the movements.

These limitations defined by the uncertainty principle or the notion of complementarity have nothing to do with the previously discussed problems based upon the role of entropy in measurements. The uncertainty is defined from a certain physical quantity h, Planck's constant. The quantity of negentropy needed for an observation is characterized by another quantity, Boltzmann's constant, k. Both discussions reveal certain limitations in our experimental methods; the influence of the coupling between the observer and the observed system is essential in both cases. The remarks made on these various examples complement each other, but quantum uncertainty cannot be reduced to the negentropy of information, nor *vice versa*.

We shall come back to these general problems later in this book.

4. CRITICISMS AND SUGGESTIONS

Looking back at these previous remarks, we feel that the problem may not have been correctly stated; many points call for further examination and discussion.

First, we assumed from the start that scientific laws contain "information," but, while using the same word as in Chapter I, we are unable to use the precise definitions introduced in Chapter I. So the question arises: what is the actual value of laws and theories, and why do we assign so much worth to their discovery?

We may risk a new suggestion here: the importance of scientific laws may very well be due to a *human factor*. Our minds like to deal with theories and general laws, rather than large accumulations of unconnected data, which we find hard to memorize. The satisfaction of discovering a general scientific law corresponds to the personal pleasure of the scientist. If, instead of a human being, we trust a machine, and let it do the scientific investigation, we immediately note that the computer does not care about theories or bare, empirical facts. It can use anything, and computes without pleasure of any sort.

When we speak of value, pleasure, or satisfaction, we definitely introduce the human element. In previous books, we emphasized repeatedly that the *problem of value* was out of reach, for the current state of information theory.

We were very cautious, in Chapter I of this book, restating these limitations very carefully. This viewpoint would make the investigation of scientific theory almost impossible. This would be, however, another exaggeration: there is undoubtedly a close connection between theories, in general, and the problem of information; but our present definitions may have to be re-examined, and the solution is not as simple as previously assumed.

Scientific laws have a special value for the *human* scientist, but they are human also in another respect: these laws are discovered by human minds; they are invented by *human imagination*. This element was clearly stated in Section 1 of this Chapter. Here again, we recognize a character which transgresses our down-to-earth definitions of Chapter I.

The first step, in a cautious examination of these difficulties, will be to discuss the exact meaning of our definition of information, and to see clearly, through some typical examples, how it can be practically used.

Information theory has proven its value in the discussion of the validity of experimental laws, since it helped in specifying some very important methods and definitions for the measurement of the "information content" of an empirical law. This problem was discussed by the present author in his book on "Science and Information Theory" (1962). As for the validity of a physical theory, two distinct points of view were successively presented by the author:

A. The physical theory may be construed as a discovery (Brillouin, 1961a) made by the human mind. It goes further than the empirical results and it seems to represent an *additional amount of information*, an actual *creation of negentropy* by human thinking.

B. The physical theory can also be considered (Brillouin, 1961b) as a work of imagination, something like a piece of poetry. It adds a great deal to the original information; some of these additions may be valuable and some of them may have no value. This point of view was presented by some very famous scientists and philosophers.

We have to compare these two different opinions, and try to figure out how much truth there may be in either of them, how far they are really in opposition, or whether they can be reconciled.

The problem is obviously on the borderline between "information theory" and "philosophy of science"; it is especially interesting to discuss this question since it is a typical example showing how far information theory (a scientific body of knowledge) can reach, and the point at which it gets difficult to apply without some new discussions.

5. The Information Content of an Empirical Law[1]

The first thing to do now is to see how far we can go by using our fundamental definition of information (I.8). We start with a simple example, corresponding to an observation under the microscope. When we look into this instrument, we see a circular field of observation; let us call P_0 the total area of this field, where we expect to find some object O. The object O does not appear as a

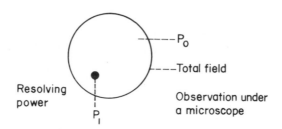

Fig. 1.

mathematical point; its image is broadened by diffraction, and covers a certain area, this area represents P_1 and yields the error in the observation. This being observed, we use our formula and define the *information*,

$$I_1 = k(\ln P_0 - \ln P_1) \tag{II.1}$$

The importance of this definition and its role in experimental physics was discussed at great length in my previous book (Brillouin, 1962).

Let us see now how a similar definition can be used for the discussion of information in connection with empirical laws.

An experiment is designed in which two variables x and y are measured. The full range of x is given by a, while b represents the full range for y. After making a number of measurements, we conclude that x and y always remain within a certain shaded strip (see Fig. 2). This accounts for a certain empirical law (dashed line) and certain limits of error $(\beta_2 - \beta_1)$.

Let $P_0 = ab$ be the area for the full range of variation of x and y while P_1 is the area of the shaded region. The amount of information is given by Eq. (1), if all regions are equally probable. In the case of unequal probabilities, a nice little mathematical problem will be raised and solved.

The similarity between the two situations shown in Figs. 1 and 2 is clear enough. In every problem encountered, it was absolutely necessary to define:

A. the *total field* (or aperture) before making the observation;

B. the *field of remaining errors* (or resolving power) after observation.

[1] Sections 5–7 are revised from excerpts from "Self-Organizing Systems" (Yovits, Jacobi, and Goldstein, eds.), p. 231, Spartan Books, Washington, D.C., 1962.

If the total field of observation is not given or if the error is not specified, the definition of "information" does not work any more, and may go up to infinity or drop to zero.

These general remarks correspond to a situation which had been emphasized many times by philosophers discussing scientific laws:

A. A scientific law always has a limited field of application.

B. It is correct "within certain possible errors."

Without both specifications A and B the statement of the law is incomplete and valueless.

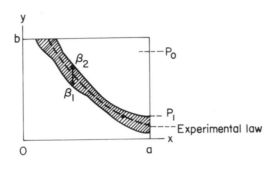

FIG. 2.

All definitions were given under the simplified assumption that the fields P_0, P_1 had sharp boundaries and uniform *a priori* probabilities in each one of them. When probabilities are not constant but vary progressively, it is a simple mathematical problem to obtain the generalization of our formula (II.1). This is discussed in the author's book (p. 6) and we do not intend to repeat here this purely mathematical discussion.

6. EXAMPLES AND DISCUSSION

We limited our discussion in the preceding section to the problem of the information contained in some empirical relations based on experiments and to summarizing their practical results.

Let us, for example, think of the famous experiments of P. W. Bridgman on high pressures. A certain piece of matter was subjected to pressures ranging from one to some thousand atmospheres. The volume of the sample was measured with limited accuracy. Here, it is obvious how to define the range of pressure (a), and the range of volume (b). Hence: $P_0 = ab$. The errors being specified, we easily compute P_1 and apply formula (II.1).

We may consider another typical case, and discuss experiments about the cross-sections for collisions of some sorts of particles. Variable x will be the momentum of the colliding particle, we may have another variable θ (deflection) to introduce, and the cross-section observed plays the role of y. Total range of variation and errors are carefully specified on $xy\theta$, and the definition of "information" is easily applied. A great variety of such examples may be found in experiments made with big accelerators.

Figure 3 exemplifies another problem. A picture is supposed to have been taken from a cloud chamber, and shows a pattern which we interpret as a collision. The raw information from this picture is simply given by the logarithm of the ratio P_0/P_1. To this, we may add some data resulting from our knowledge of experimental conditions in the machine. Any information computed from this raw material must be smaller than the raw information itself.

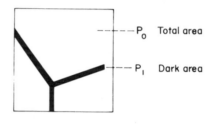

FIG. 3.

Let us now remind the reader of the fact that *experimental errors* are unavoidable (Brillouin, 1959). Many physicists still believe that these errors can be considered as a secondary effect, a sheer nuisance that could be neglected and should be ignored by the theory. The old assumption was that errors could be made as small as might be desired by careful instrumentation and were not essential. This is an unrealistic scheme, which has been washed away by modern physics. There are many causes for experimental errors, and they very often cannot be corrected.

The importance of thermal agitation is now well known; it results in Brownian motion in all pieces of equipment, thermal noise, etc., and this kind of perturbation can only be reduced by cooling the whole apparatus to very low temperatures.

An experiment is always supposed to be built in such a way that it be completely isolated from any outside influence. But this is often a dream, and many unknown effects from far away cannot be shielded. E. Borel (1912) once pointed out that a motion of 1 gram of matter by 1 cm on a not too distant star (say, Sirius) would make a change of about 10^{-100} in the gravitation field on the earth. Then he figured out that a change of 10^{-100} in the initial positions and velocities of the molecules of a gas would make it impossible to compute the motion of these molecules for more than one millionth of a second.

The present author, in many publications, has repeatedly emphasized the essential role of errors: if you gain an amount of information ΔI, by making a certain experiment, it will be paid for by an increase of entropy $\Delta S \geq \Delta I$ somewhere in the apparatus. It is thus unthinkable to avoid errors and make ΔI infinite. M. Born (1955) starting from a different point of view, reached very similar conclusions.

7. How Is Science Actually Being Built?

The Meaning of an Experiment

First of all, an experiment is entirely different from a simple random observation. The researcher asks himself a question, which results from his previous scientific knowledge; this question is aimed at checking certain predictions, or it must prepare the way for the discovery of new facts. The question must be stated with precision, and apply to a problem which *may be isolated from the outside world*. It is imperative that the experimental apparatus be protected from unknown perturbations which would disturb the observation and the results.

At any rate, these conditions represent the ideal hoped for by a physicist or a chemist, an ideal which is not always realized, and is sometimes even unrealizable. The astronomer cannot isolate one star from the rest of the universe, but he reasons "as if" this isolation could be obtained. He isolates the observation "in his thought," evidently a very precarious process. In geology, in the science of life, and in sociology, the isolation is infeasible, and the isolation "in thought" becomes extremely dubious. The physico-chemist is a favored experimenter, an extreme example worth studying. He chooses his problem, isolates his apparatus, protects it against all outside perturbations. If it is feasible, he repeats the experiment a number of times, and checks the isolation of the apparatus through the concordance of repeated observations. The strict concordance of the observed results is an unrealizable fiction. It is impossible, even with the best isolated apparatus in the world, to avoid accidental errors of observation and all sorts of unpredictable perturbations. Empirical results are therefore represented by a law of probabilities, and are translated into statistical rules of distribution. If the differences remain small, the scientist computes *a mean value*, which characterizes the measurements made, and indicates the variation, the likely error which must be taken into account in the observation.

After these general remarks, it is necessary to mention the limitations imposed by Heisenberg's uncertainty conditions. To isolate the experiment from the rest of the world is not sufficient; isolation should also be established between the observer and his apparatus, but this isolation cannot be complete, for that would preclude all possibility of observation. Therefore, a certain coupling between observer and apparatus cannot be avoided, and this is taken care of by Heisenberg's conditions.

The freedom of the scientist is essential for the choice of the research topic and of the experimental method to be used. No calculating machine can make this choice, which requires reflection, and a real perspicacity on the part of the researcher. After long reflection, the physicist may use the machine to compute the optimum conditions, and weigh the relative importance of the various factors. The machine is a tool, an auxiliary, but nothing more. To compute is not to think.

A typical example is the famous negative experiment made by Michelson, Morley, and Miller on the "ether wind." Miller wanted to observe this ether wind and he built a highly precise apparatus, on a California mountain (Sommerfeld, 1954). He observed rather disorderly deviations, from which he drew not very convincing conclusions. Later checks proved that the terrain was unstable and cut through by multiple cracks in the rocks, originating from very ancient earthquakes. Similar experiments taken up again later by Joos in an underground concrete laboratory, very stable, yielded frankly negative results, and proved without discussion the validity of relativity.

8. EMPIRICAL AND THEORETICAL LAWS

The general procedure discussed in Section 5 can be used for any kind of law used to summarize a certain number of experimental results. The law may be purely empirical and be expressed by graphs or numerical tables. It can be based on a theory and show the accuracy with which the theory checks with experiments. It does not make any difference at this stage. Given

(A) the range of use of the formula (initial uncertainty P_0) and

(B) the errors, hence the final uncertainty P_1,

we measure the total information with Eq. (I.8) or (II.1).

The theory does not seem to play any role in this problem. The scientist may be proud of the theory he has been clever enough tó build up, but this pride (a typical human value) does not appear in our estimates of information.

An engineer, using a large-scale computer for the discussion of a purely technical problem, does not care whether any theory may exist to prove the formula he is using. He is only interested in the limits A and B; they represent all he needs in his job.

The theory, it appears, plays a role when we want to compare different experimental laws and to discover any interconnections among them. Theory is important because of the *correlations* it helps to formulate. This may be accounted for in the following example, which represents a very crude scheme, but one that can serve as a basis for a precise mathematical discussion. Let us assume that we start with a few empirical laws, α, β, γ, and compute their information content I_α, I_β, I_γ. These laws being discovered independently, the total information of the set of laws is

$$I_{tot} = I_\alpha + I_\beta + I_\gamma \qquad (II.2)$$

Then, we happen to discover a theory that produces interconnections among these three laws. When we take the results of the first law (α), they already contain some suggestions about the second law (β). In other words, when (α) is given, the field $P'_{0\beta}$ of variation for β is reduced, and is smaller than the total $P_{0\beta}$ for a completely arbitrary variation (Fig. 4). We thus obtain less information when we consider β.

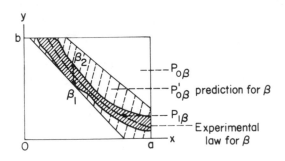

FIG. 4.

$$I'_\beta = k \ln \frac{P'_{0\beta}}{P_{1\beta}} < I_\beta = k \ln \frac{P_{0\beta}}{P_{1\beta}} \qquad (II.3)$$

Again, when we know (α) and (β), we discover that the field of variation of (γ) is very much reduced, and a measurement of (γ) yields much less information, $I'_\gamma < I_\gamma$. We finally have the following situation:

$$I_{tot} = I_\alpha + I_\beta + I_\gamma = I_\alpha + I'_\beta + I'_\gamma + R \qquad (II.4)$$

with a positive residue R. The oversimplified scheme explained in this example corresponds to the theory of *redundancy* developed by Shannon [see the author's book "Science and Information Theory" (1956, 1962, Chapters 3–5)].

"Redundancy" is just another name for *interconnection* or *correlation*; the amount of information contained in the correlation is represented by R in Eq. (II.4). This method provides us with a definition of the *information contained in the theory* correlating the laws (α), (β), and (γ).

A precise mathematical formulation requires much more elaborate probability discussions; but the essential points are already there in our simplified example.

The theory has a beauty, an aesthetic value, for the scientist, but we do not see how to account for this factor. We can, however, measure the correlation provided by the theory, and this is of great philosophical importance.

9. THE CONDITIONS FOR AN IDEAL THEORY

The conditions we want to define are those corresponding to the limiting case of an ideal theory, something that would correspond to classical mechanics or to classical electromagnetism, within their classical domain of application and with the usual experimental errors. Such an *ideal* theory is supposed to have been developed in a very general way, but it still contains a few arbitrary data such as masses, charges, initial conditions of particles used in a special problem, together with boundary conditions, etc.

All these arbitrary quantities might be "given" by the theoretician, but this is an unrealistic situation which we want to exclude. The quantities are *given* at an examination, when the teacher states a problem to his students, but in actual scientific research, the quantities *result* from previous sets of measurements and experimental observations. We assume all these previous observations to be contained in the first empirical law α of Eq. (II.2).

When these initial observations have been made, with some corresponding errors, the ideal theory is supposed to be able to predict the correct answer to the problem, together with expected errors.

This means that further experiments, β, γ, . . . should bring nothing new. According to our definitions this situation can be expressed by the relation

$$P'_{0\beta} = P_{1\beta} \qquad P'_{0\gamma} = P_{1\gamma} \tag{II.5}$$

no new information:

$$I'_{\beta} = 0 \qquad I'_{\gamma} = 0$$

In Fig. 4, the two shaded regions would coincide, and experimental errors $(P_{1\beta})$ should just extend over the region of expected errors $(P_{0\beta})$. Such conditions represent the *perfect check of theory and experiment*. Referring now to Eqs. (II.4) we obtain

$$R = I_{\text{tot}} - I_{\alpha} = I_{\text{theor}} \tag{II.6}$$

The quantity R represents the information contained in the theory, and it finally amounts to

$$I_{\text{theor}} = I_{\beta} + I_{\gamma} \ldots = \sum (\text{predictable information}) \tag{II.7}$$

The *ideal theory* yields total information which is just equal to the sum of the information that normally would have been contained in all the empirical results, which are now safely predicted by theoretical calculations.

In other words, we may summarize the *theoretical information* for an *"ideal theory"* by the usual formula

$$I = k \ln \frac{P_{0 \text{ theor}}}{P_{1 \text{ theor}}} \tag{II.8}$$

where $P_{0 \text{ theor}}$ is the extension of the domain over which the theory is valid, and $P_{1 \text{ theor}}$ represents the expected errors.

We thus end up, for this very important problem, with a formula exactly similar to our initial formula (II.1).

A remarkable thing is that these methods and definitions do not leave any margin for any "information" resulting from the work of the computing theoretician, and no reward for his skill.

This is definitely a limitation of our fundamental assumptions: they do not yield any practical result for pure mathematical problems. They implicitly assume that the scientist is a perfect mathematician and uses faultless computing machines.

Given the initial data, the final results are supposed to be automatically known. This is obviously a very extreme oversimplification, and the whole problem of an information theory applicable to pure mathematics remains wide open.

The case of *computing* is similar to the problem of *translating*: an ideal translator adds no information, and *loses none*, but simply makes a foreign language understandable to us (Brillouin, 1962, p. 268).

These assumptions may look arbitrary, but they are consistent with our position that information is negative entropy. A perfect translation must be reversible and introduces no entropy change (no information gain nor loss). A perfect computation is exactly in the same position. These remarks agree with deductions made by the logicians Carnap and Bar-Hillel (Brillouin, 1962, p. 298).

10. IMPORTANCE AND VALUE OF THEORIES

The scheme presented in the preceding sections is obviously oversimplified, but it seems fundamentally correct; the corresponding definitions could easily be generalized for more complex situations, and the general theory of redundancy, developed by Shannon, would provide the necessary mathematical tools.

Let us try, at this point, to explain again our position about the importance and value of theories for experimental sciences. In another chapter, we shall discuss the fundamental differences between mathematics and the experimental sciences.

The importance of theories may be specified as consisting of different (and sometimes contradictory) elements.

A. *Practical value:* the theory enables us to make *predictions*; this proves that it actually contains some real information.

B. *Aesthetic value:* the scientist takes pride in the beauty of the theory he has been able to design. It gives him the pleasant feeling of understanding and *comprehension*. Note that the original etymologic meaning of this last word was: to take together (cum-prehend), to regroup and assemble together. The discussion in Section 8 was based upon this remark, which was translated into mathematical formulas.

Let us now examine both characteristics A and B.

A. Let us assume that a theory has been found and tested experimentally over a certain domain, in a great many circumstances. We feel that it is reasonably valid over this general domain, and we use the theory for making predictions. Note that the previous tests did *not* cover all the possible situations in the domain of application. What we actually do is known as *interpolation* or *extrapolation*. In the first case, we feel relatively safe. Interpolation is usually correct. As for extrapolation, it certainly is a rather hazardous procedure. We try to extend the theory to the limits of the domain and to discover the boundaries beyond which the theory cannot be used any more. These limits depend, of course, upon the approximations we are satisfied with.

For instance, let us consider classical mechanics. The boundaries of its domain are defined by the conditions (small dimensions, so that the duration of propagation with velocity c can be safely neglected):

$$v << c \quad \text{velocities much lower than the velocity} \qquad \text{(II.5)}$$
$$\text{of light, } c$$

$$h\nu << E \quad \text{low frequencies } \nu, \text{ with quantum } h\nu \text{ much} \qquad \text{(II.6)}$$
$$\text{smaller than energy } E$$

The condition (II.5) is needed to remain far from relativity. The second condition, (II.6), keeps us far from quantum theory, and makes it reasonable to use continuous variables, instead of dealing with quantum jumps.

The exact limits can be computed if we decide upon the approximation we are ready to accept. For instance, if we assume that we can tolerate an error of 10^{-10} we have to state

$$\frac{v^2}{c^2} < 10^{-10} \qquad v < 10^{-5}c \qquad \text{(II.7)}$$

for the first condition (II.5). A similar discussion should be had for the second condition (II.6), to specify how small the energy E may be. Condition (II.7) yields an upper limit for the velocity v and the condition on E would fix a lower limit on E, hence a lower limit for kinetic energy and velocity. Finally, our domain will be defined by some condition

$$v_{min} < v < 10^{-5}c \qquad \text{(II.8)}$$

New experiments may increase our information, either by increasing the domain of application, or by decreasing experimental errors.

B. The aesthetic value of a theory has been admired many times by a large number of scientists. Einstein repeatedly emphasized the importance of mathematical beauty in a physical theory. He even indulged candidly in admiring the beautiful structure of the universe, while, in our opinion, the actual aesthetic greatness was in his theory, more than in the universe at large: this universe is much more complicated than the remarkable model of cosmogony invented by Einstein, a model capable of representing only the average behavior of the universe, but not all the details of its structure. The feeling of understanding is first a feeling of pleasure and satisfaction; but it goes beyond that, and makes available to the scientist an intuitive grasp and the possibility of direct prediction, even when detailed computation does not seem practical.

A theory which our brain is able to understand and to adapt to its own logical methods plays the role of a good translation from a mysterious language into a language we know. It enables us to follow our usual lines of reasoning, to use our standard methods of thinking, and to apply them to the discussion of the phenomena in the universe around us. The translation may be only partly correct. It may apply only to a certain domain of the universe. Nevertheless, it is extremely useful to the scientist, who has a feeling of leaving a wild unknown country to enter a civilized world, with roads and rules he can accept and follow safely; but he should never forget that these roads—as well as a good deal of the landscaping surrounding them—are man made and that the wild forest cannot be very far off.

REFERENCES

Borel, E. (1912). "Introduction géométrique à la physique." Gauthier-Villars, Paris.

Born, M. (1955). Continuity, determinism and reality. *Kgl. Danske Videnskab. Selskab. Mat. Fys. Medd.* **30**, No. 2.

Brillouin, L. (1956). "Science and Information Theory," 1st ed. Academic Press, New York.

Brillouin, L. (1959). Information theory and its applications to fundamental problems in physics. *Nature* **183**, 501.

Brillouin, L. (1961a). Thermodynamics, statistics and information. *Am. J. Phys.* **29**, 326–327.

Brillouin, L. (1961b). Science and imagination. *Nouvelle Rev. Franç.*

Brillouin, L. (1962). "Science and Information Theory," 2nd ed., Chapter 20, p. 289. Academic Press, New York.

Sommerfeld, A. (1954). "Lectures on Theoretical Physics," Vol. 4: Optics, p. 75. Academic Press, New York.

Chapter III

MATHEMATICAL THEOREMS AND PHYSICAL THEORIES

1. Necessary Distinction between Mathematics and the Physical Sciences

The theory of information raises a number of fundamental questions about the first postulates of science and the limits of their validity. As an example of such problems, let us examine the opinions of a pure mathematician and of a physicist about the foundations of geometry. The mathematician starts with dimensionless points, infinitely thin curves and surfaces, and continuous space-time. Atomic science denies any real meaning to these definitions.

Consider a very thin piece of tinfoil, and look at it with X-rays: you discover an atomic lattice, with isolated atoms separated by large, empty intervals. The foil has a finite thickness and is not continuous. Even a monomolecular layer exhibits similar properties.

There is absolutely no possibility for measuring a distance much smaller than 10^{-15} cm, simply because there is no yardstick available for such small orders of magnitude. Let us suppose one would like to measure 10^{-50} cm. The only length standard he could use would be a wavelength λ of a comparable order of length. Whether he chooses light or any kind of De Broglie or Dirac wave would not make much difference. The energy quanta would be of the order of magnitude:

$$E = h\nu = h\frac{c}{\lambda} \approx \frac{2\cdot10^{-16}}{10^{-50}} = 2\cdot10^{34} \text{ C.G.S.} \qquad \text{(III.1)}$$

This represents a fantastic amount of energy, capable of blowing to pieces the laboratory and the whole earth. Let us use Einstein's relation to compute the mass M that could be totally annihilated at one single stroke:

$Mc^2 = E$

$$M = \frac{2 \cdot 10^{34}}{9 \cdot 10^{20}} \approx 2 \cdot 10^{13} \text{ grams} = 2 \cdot 10^{10} \text{ kg} = 2 \cdot 10^7 \text{ metric tons} \qquad (\text{III.2})$$

Every interaction between such a wave and any physical system would involve at least one such quantum, either absorbed or emitted, and provoke an immediate catastrophy.

Needless to say, this short computation is sufficient to prove the absolute impossibility of measuring 10^{-50} cm; and if he cannot measure it, a physicist will never dare speak of it.

A mathematician goes ahead without even noticing the obstacle; he simply ignores it completely.

The mathematician very carefully defines irrational numbers. The physicist never meets any such numbers. Whatever he measures is represented by a finite number, with so many figures, and a certain amount of uncertainty. The mathematician shudders at uncertainty and tries to ignore experimental errors.

Open a book of pure mathematics and consider a theorem. It is always built on a typical scheme: given certain conditions, A, B, C, which are assumed to be exactly fulfilled, it can be proven rigorously that conclusion Q must be true. Here the physicist starts wondering: how can we know that A, B, C are *exactly* fulfilled? No observation can tell us that much. The only thing we may know is that A, B, C are approximately satisfied within certain limits of error. Then, what does the theorem prove? Very small errors of A, B, or C may result in a very small error of the final statement Q, or they may destroy it completely. The discussion is not complete until the problem of the stability of the theorem has been investigated, and this is another story!

2. Basic Formulations in Mathematics

Historically, mathematics was originally a codification of experimental observations, but it emerged progressively as an independent body of knowledge. Geometry was started as a set of rules for measuring land, to be used by surveyors. It ranged near geology and geography, but now the point of view has been reversed and geometry is supposed to be based on a system of postulates, with no reference to their physical meaning. Classical mechanics had been organized in a similar way, but it could not be kept in such a straitjacket. An "agonizing reappraisal" had to be made, a choice between mathematical logic and physical application; physical experiments exploded the rigid armor of strict mathematics.

During the past few centuries, philosophers took a traditional approach to scientific problems. They assumed theoretical geometry to represent perfect scientific knowledge, with mechanics approaching perfection, and physics not very far from it. This childish pattern cannot be maintained nowadays, and we must emphasize the fundamental structural difference between mathematics and physical (or chemical and biological) theories.

There is a wide gulf between both methods, and the gulf is widening every day. Atomic bombs and space travel are making it impossible to bridge the gap.

The typical mathematical method can be summarized as follows: it starts first with some general ideas and schemes suggested by observation, but it soon forgets about this first origin, and proceeds to oversimplification, reducing the point of departure to a set of dreary postulates and dry specifications of the rules to be applied; no reference is made to any empirical result. Even logical methods are defined without any strict similarity to usual logic, the only limitations are contained in proofs of "completeness" and "lack of contradictions" in the basic definitions. From there on, reasoning can proceed on and on—with no discussion of the practical value, nor of possible applications.

It is akin to scholastic casuistry, and claims at absolute certainty. It might very well be described as the first of the "*nonobjective*" *arts*, and attracts the admiration of many poets. The famous French poet Paul Valery confessed his great respect for abstract geometry: its weightless architecture, built with cold logic and strict rigidity fascinated him. He admired the unreal magic of its absolute irresponsibility.

A textbook on mathematics appears as a succession of lemmas, theorems, and corollaries; it reads like an epic poem divided into strophes, stanzas, and verses. This wonderful organization looks very impressive, but it is mostly artificial. The artist in mathematics first discovers some curious relationships, new properties that seem disconnected; step by step, he manages to assemble these bits of knowledge, and to group them logically, according to the standard fashion, into a succession of theorems. This is the mathematical style, the art of writing, which was adopted by Spinoza in his "Ethics," for philosophical problems.

A mathematical theory sets no limit on its domain of applicability, and does not shudder at defining infinity. If the domain is infinite, so also is the accuracy. Let us try to speak of *information* according to our previous definitions: the domain P_0 is infinite, the point P_1 is just 1, and

$$\text{Information} \quad I = k \ln \frac{P_0}{P_1} = k \ln \infty = \infty \quad \text{(III.3)}$$

Demonstrations, proofs, new theorems, etc., cannot modify the result. One assumes infinite information at the start, and whatever one does cannot change it. This strange result has already been noted by some famous mathematicians. Carnap and Bar-Hillel stated this paradox very clearly (see Brillouin, 1956, 1962, Chapter 20, p. 298).

3. THE VIEWPOINT OF EXPERIMENTAL SCIENTISTS

The mathematician dreams of measurements of infinite accuracy, defining, for instance, the position of a point without any possible error. It would mean an experiment yielding an infinite amount of information, and this is physically impossible. One of the most important results of information theory is known as the "negentropy principle of information." It states that any information obtained from an experiment must be paid for in negentropy. As D. Gabor states it: "You cannot get something for nothing, not even an observation." If an experiment yields information ΔI, there must have been increase of entropy

$$\Delta S \geq \Delta I \tag{III.4}$$

in the apparatus or in the laboratory where the experiment was performed. An increase ΔS in entropy means a decrease

$$\Delta N = -\Delta S \tag{III.5}$$

in the total "negentropy." The information ΔI is paid for by a larger amount ΔN of negentropy.

$$\Delta N + \Delta I \leq 0 \tag{III.6}$$

A very large amount of information will cost a very high price, and an infinite amount of information is unattainable. No wealth could pay for it. Another important point refers more specifically to the definition of a continuum in space–time. The discussion sketched in the first section of this chapter is carefully examined (L. Brillouin, 1956 or 1962, Chapter 16) and leads to the result that the measurement of a very small length Δx (and by "very small," a length smaller than 10^{-13} cm is meant) requires the use of a total energy ΔE such that

$$\Delta E \Delta x \geq \tfrac{1}{2}hc \tag{III.7}$$

This represents a new limitation, different from the uncertainty principle, and completely independent of the conditions specified in Eq. (III.4). Extremely small distances cannot be measured, unless a source of very high energy is used. This energy may not be completely dissipated, but it is needed for the experiment.

Both results lead to similar conclusions: an infinite amount of information can never be obtained. An infinitely small distance cannot be measured. Geometrical and mathematical definitions are only dreams which the physicist cannot trust, and we should especially emphasize the impossibility of physically defining a continuum in space and time.

We emphasized in Section 1 of this Chapter the complete lack of significance of irrational numbers for a physicist. Irrational numbers are supposed to be known with infinite accuracy—one hundred, one million, or one billion decimal places are not enough. All this is absolutely meaningless for an experimenter; he can measure to five decimal places, or maybe ten decimal places, but there is not a single experiment that may yield twenty decimal places. It does not make sense to ask whether the velocity of light c be a rational number, or whether the ratio M/m of proton mass M to electron mass m may be rational. All irrational numbers, like π, e, $\sqrt{2}$, etc., result only from abstract mathematical definitions; but, as we said, mathematics is nonobjective art. No physical object can display real geometrical properties to the limit assumed by mathematicians; we may even call it "wishful thinking."

4. THE OPINION OF MAX BORN

It is not necessary to repeat here many more comments and explanations. Let us recall only that the negentropy principle of information gives a precise meaning to an old remark of J. von Neumann who says that an observation is an irreversible process. Condition (III.4) specifies the amount of irreversibility.

It may be interesting to quote another author, Max Born, and to discuss a series of papers he recently published. In the Jubilee Volume (Born, 1955) presented to Niels Bohr on his seventieth birthday, under the title, "Continuity, Determinism and Reality," Max Born presents some general remarks very close to ours, although his line of reasoning is different:

> I maintain that the mathematical concept of a point in a continuum has no direct physical significance. It has no meaning to say that a coordinate x... has a value $x = \sqrt{2}$ inch or $x = \pi$ cm.

[This disposes of irrational numbers!]

> Modern physics has achieved its greatest successes by applying the methodological principle that concepts which refer to distinctions beyond possible experience have no physical meaning and ought to be eliminated. ... The most glaringly successful cases are Einstein's foundation of relativity based on the rejection of the concept of ether ... and Heisenberg's foundation of quantum mechanics. ... *I think that this principle should be applied also to the idea of physical continuity.*

Max Born also explains that experimental errors should be taken into account right from the beginning, in the field of classical physics, where they have been too often ignored.

He does not want to reject the mathematical concept of a real number, but specifies that "the situation demands a description of haziness." The probability for the value of a physical quantity to be in a given interval should be specified, instead of pretending that the value of the quantity can be known exactly.

Born came back to these problems in further papers, and, finally, in a most interesting report (1961) published in the Jubilee Volume dedicated to W. Heisenberg on his sixtieth birthday. He refers to some recent papers of the present author, and finds himself in complete agreement with our point of view. The reader will find, in this last paper, a number of important remarks.

Many examples discussed by Born ought to be given here, but we hope the reader will refer to the original papers.

Let us remember that the general principle invoked by Born is often quoted as Bridgman's *operational* point of view.

5. THE EXPERIMENTAL CUSTOMER IS ALWAYS RIGHT

A few examples may help to specify more clearly the opposition between mathematics and theoretical physics. The vivid contrast will thus appear in full light.

A mathematical theory can be built on any set of definitions, however arbitrary or fantastic they might be. The only conditions are the lack of internal contradiction, and a logical structure.

A physical theory is usually based on a few selected experimental results, which are not always too well defined from a mathematician's viewpoint. These results are first oversimplified and codified for introduction into a model that may contain a good deal of additional human invention springing from the scientist's imagination, and not from direct experimental facts. On this basis, not too precisely nor logically specified, a theoretical system is built, and predictions are made. The catch is: Are these predictions checked by experiments with sufficient accuracy? If so, the theory is good, at least as a point of departure, and it can be more efficiently developed. Otherwise, the whole system is just good for the waste basket.

Let us go back to the year 1913, when this author was a student at Munich. A most important problem for theoreticians, at that time, was the junction of Einstein's first theory of relativity with the theory of gravitation (universal attraction). Einstein stated a maximum velocity c for the propagation of any physical property, while universal attraction had been assumed by Newton to spread instantly at any distance. A famous German theoretician, G. Mie, proposed a very ingenious solution, introducing two different definitions for "inertial mass" m_i and "gravitational mass" m_g. Both masses were assumed practically equal at low velocities, but they differed at high velocities. The theory was a little marvel, and so interesting in its logical structure that A. Sommerfeld spent two lectures discussing it in great detail. However, it was a failure. Experiments did not verify any prediction. Nobody now remembers the Mie theory; Einstein's generalized relativity was based on the assumption of a single mass, and met with all difficulties.

There are hundreds of such examples. Many physicists and engineers attempted to write Maxwell's equations in a completely symmetrical way, with single magnetic poles (the so-called mono-poles) corresponding to single electric charges. This simply does not check, even when it happens to be revived by a famous theoretician. Maxwell's equations are not completely symmetrical.

Biochemistry is not completely symmetrical either, and optical rotations play a fundamental role, as emphasized by Pasteur. Even elementary particles exhibit strange dissymmetries, and this was discovered by Lee and Yang. Symmetries are really appealing, but they are exceptional in actual observation.

Perfect logic and faultless deduction make a pleasant theoretical structure, but it may be right or wrong; the experimenter is the only one to decide, and he is always right.

In connection with the problems discussed in this Chapter, the reader will be interested in the penetrating discussion of L. Tisza (1963), where he will find many valuable remarks that show great similarity to our viewpoint.

To summarize the whole discussion of this Chapter, one might say that a mathematical theory is built from certain premises upward, while a physical interpretation is erected in order to reach some final results. Mathematics starts from the basement, and theoretical physics wants to obtain given experimental facts, at the top of the whole structure.

REFERENCES

Born, M. (1953). Physical reality. *Phil. Quart.* **3**, 139.

Born, M. (1955). Continuity, determinism and reality. *Kgl. Danske Videnskab Selskab. Mat. fys. Medd.* **30**, No. 2.

Born, M. (1961). Bemerkungen zur statistischen Deutung der Quantenmechanik. In the Jubilee Volume "Werner Heisenberg und die Physik unserer Zeit," pp. 103–118. Vieweg, Braunschweig.

Brillouin, L. (1956). "Science and Information Theory," 1st ed. Academic Press, New York.

Brillouin, L. (1962). "Science and Information Theory," 2nd ed. Academic Press, New York.

Tisza, L. (1963). *Rev. Modern Phys.* **35**, 151–184.

Chapter IV

IMAGINATION AND INVENTION IN A THEORY

1. The Birth of a Scientific Law[1]

Too many laymen picture science as a sheer accumulation of facts, and take a scientist for a living encyclopedia. They think it possible to solve every problem by means of giant machines which might register all human knowledge in their enormous, magnetic memories. Do you need some information? Push a button and the machine will answer! This is ridiculous, and stems from the poorest science fiction. More important, it proves that the role of the scientist is too often completely misunderstood.

Let us examine how a scientific law is actually discovered. Nature, taken as a whole, in its integrity, is much too complex and goes beyond our comprehension. We have to analyze it, divide it into its components, explain its working parts, and examine them one by one. This is what we do when we try to isolate portions which can be separated, and which we then observe methodically, piecemeal.

These observations, first made bit by bit, then classified and patched together, yield a raw material, which we call information (Brillouin, 1962). Then comes the research of scientific laws. This is a delicate abstraction to analyze where very differing elements come in:

A. A summary of observed facts.

B. Various models (mechanical, electrical, atomic, etc.), used as a basis for reasoning.

C. *Imagination*, presenting a variety of possible conclusions for these models.

[1] Sections 1–4 revised from excerpts from "Self-Organizing Systems" (Yovits, Jacobi, and Goldstein, eds.), p. 231, Spartan Books, Washington, D.C., 1962.

    D. Choice of one model, and discussion of the laws and consequences which might result from it.

    E. Among all the possible choices, *the search for simplicity*. It has been often said that "nature is simple"—illusion! It is our mind which *looks* for simplicity, to avoid effort.

    F. Verification; more or less exact concordance of the proposed law, when checked with experimental facts.

All these steps deserve examination and discussion. We do not pretend to be able to exhaust such a problem; we are only trying to state it. Especially, we want to underline the part played by the human mind in this process. *A physical law* is not solely a summary of empirical results. Such a summary, represented by curves, plots, and computing tables, corresponds to nothing more than the work of an empirical engineer, of a technician refusing to deviate from the facts, and not looking for an interpretation or complete *understanding*.

The latter word has been said, but what does it mean? When will we be able to say that we understand a physical phenomenon? We get this satisfying impression when we have been able to imagine a *model* which, using accepted laws, can supply us with an "explanation" of the results observed in a new series of experiments. To understand is to come back to what has "already been seen."

Note that the term *model* covers a vast variety of configurations. It can be a mechanism or an electrical model, or it can be a system of equations (the electromagnetism of Maxwell), in short, any representation enabling us to do some reasoning.

Finally, this model is limited in its aims, just like the experiments it is expected to sum up. The laws *imagined by the scientists* yield results which are *correct within certain limits*.

If we attempt to extrapolate them too far, we discover divergences; the law has to be revised and corrected, and this revision very often requires some radical changes in the model.

2. A SCIENTIFIC LAW IS AN INTERPRETATION OF NATURE BY HUMAN THOUGHT

Absolute freedom of thought is essential. Any preimposed theoretical system (Marxism, Religion, Materialism, Positivism or Machinism) is an obstacle and a hindrance.

Let us insist that it is an irresponsible exaggeration to speak of the laws of nature as if these laws did actually exist in the absence of man. Such a childish point of view may have been accepted in old times, but modern scientists have had to abandon it in recent years, for many serious reasons. First, the complexity of nature makes it impossible for our mind to embrace it in its totality. As we said before, we artifically split it into fragments, and observe it piecemeal. The laws we discover are dependent upon the type of splitting used, and we always have to correct them afterwards, in order to account for the inevitable coupling among the parts we have taken apart in our discussion. Not only is the whole a sum of the pieces, but also a very complex system of actions and reactions may modify very seriously the laws applicable to the ensemble. Every time scientists tried to generalize too fast some laws observed on a certain scale, they stumbled over unexpected road blocks, and had to revise their whole system of rules.

The main role of *human imagination* in the invention (we intentionally do not use the term "discovery") and the formulation of scientific laws is illustrated by numerous examples. Let us recall the history of mechanics:

A. Newton invents laws of mechanics, and imagines the laws of instantaneous universal attraction.

B. Faced with new experiments, Einstein discards the Newton model, and searches for a new "model of the universe," capable of giving an account of all the facts. His imagination suggests relativity to him, as well as the four-dimensional time-space.

C. At the same time, Planck invents the quantum to represent the laws of radiation. Soon after, N. Bohr invents an atomic model.

D. Louis de Broglie and E. Schrödinger invent wave mechanics.

E. M. Born and W. Heisenberg imagine the mechanics of matrices, and these two models, which seem to contradict each other, are finally linked, thanks to the introduction of statistical laws. This result is hardly reached, when a new quantity has to be added, the spin of the electron, which enables us to classify (it would be exaggerated to say "understand") a whole series of strange peculiarities of atoms.

The mechanics of ultimate particles is only beginning to take shape; we are surprised every day by new experimental results and *our imagination does not manage* to follow this infernal race.

As soon as we abandon the familiar ground of terrestrial experiments practiced on a human scale upon inaminate objects, our mind is suddenly faced with incomprehensible facts. The role of the imagination then becomes preponderant: astronomy, geology, ultimate particles or nuclei, finally biology—in all these fields strict logic is no longer sufficient. Down-to-earth reasoning fails, and imagination rules.

3. BRIDGMAN'S OPERATIONAL METHOD

We must now consider the viewpoint repeatedly emphasized by Bridgman: the only physical quantities are those which can be measured, and for which a measuring operation can be stated. Things that cannot be observed and measured have no actual physical existence. They are creations of our imagination; they can be useful and help our visualization, but they have no real physical meaning. They may play an important role in one model, and be thrown overboard in another model. Remember how "ether" was erased and discarded by Einstein's relativity. In short, "Beware of imagination!"

The operational method is a very safe guide. We should never take too seriously the additional quantities introduced in any model by our imagination. This sound advice, however, is very difficult to follow. We always put into our models much more than the bare facts; otherwise, there would be no model!

Here we come to the fundamental question: How much information does a theory contain? Conversely, how much of the theory is sheer imagination? We raised the question in the introduction, and we now have to discuss it.

Many scientists have a tendency to believe in theory more than in experimental facts. A theory represents an organized body of knowledge, easy to remember and ready for application. Moreover, the theory pretends to be rigorous. It is often taught as a piece of mathematics, based on some axioms and rules, and able to give a strictly exact answer to any question.

If this were true, we could accept the statement given in Chapter II, Sections 1 and 2: "When Einstein formulated the principle of relativity, and when de Broglie invented wave mechanics, these thinkers really created new processes of scientific prediction. They supplied humanity with information up to then unknown. From these remarks, we can draw the following suggestion: thought creates negative entropy."

This conclusion may, however, be too hasty and should be carefully weighed. The inventor of a new theory (or a new model) is inclined to think that his theory is absolutely correct and general. Other scientists usually are more skeptical and look for practical results, predicted by the theory, that might be checked in the laboratory. This research ends up with a number of new laws, more or less verified by experiments, within certain limits of error. Sooner or later, some of the predictions will be found incorrect. Altogether, scientists finally discover:

A. The limits of applicability of a certain theory with its field of successful prediction, and where it starts to fail. This enables one to compute P_0.

B. The limits of errors in experimental checks over the field of successful application; from this we obtain P_1.

The discussion of A and B finally gives a possibility for computing the ratio P_0/P_1 and the amount of *correct* information contained in the theory. Hence we conclude:

A given mathematical theory is a rigorous structure, valid over any field and without any limitation. When this theory is used as a *physical model*, it is subject to both limitations A and B and some allowance for errors must be introduced before it can be applied to physics. The rigorous mathematical theory would mean an infinite amount of information. The physical theory, with the A–B limitations, yields a finite amount of information.

The present author has been able to watch a great many attempts at building new physical theories. He is in a position to remember how many of these inventions failed definitely, how many succeeded, and how they all had to be later modified and corrected. Some of the theories proposed were little marvels of ingenuity, but they were failures. Some attempts looked very crude and unsatisfactory, but they proved to be a step in the right direction and wound up as most important discoveries (think of quantum theory).

As for the complete change of model required to make, at first sight, just a tiny correction in the results, we have many good examples. The most famous ones are represented by:

Classical Mechanics → Special Relativity → General Relativity

These radical changes of models resulted in a stupendous expansion of the field of action (P_0 increased, information increased). The reader may easily convince himself of the truth contained in the preceding discussion: a brilliant piece of theory is just a wonderful dream, a splendid poetical essay. If the dream comes true, if poetry checks with facts, then it becomes a piece of information.

4. SCIENTIFIC THEORIES ARE BORN IN OUR IMAGINATION

We could multiply the examples. Modern physics is full of bizarre interpretations, but the chosen models, no matter how strange they might appear, are in close concordance with the facts.

We used to imagine that there was a real universe, outside of us, which could persist even when we stopped observing it. However, (quoting M. Planck), we must immediately add: "This real, outside world is not directly perceptible to us." We replace it with a *physical model of the world* (*ein physikalisches Weltbild*), which is more or less adapted to observations.

"Real nature!" This formulation resembles "nature in itself," the "essence" of phenomena—and other dangerous scholastic expressions. The scientist, without admitting it, very often uses metaphysical ideas which play an important role in his thinking. He tries not to be hampered by them, but does not always manage to ignore them.

Nature exceeds our imagination, as long as the latter remains too strictly tied to our everyday vision of the world. The simplest models, drawn from our experience, on a human scale, are not acceptable for the interpretation of atomic and subatomic facts. Something else must be invented: abstract symbols, impossible to represent simply, have to be played upon; words have to be created; and the scientist coins a scientific jargon, a bric-a-brac of contradictory notions, transposed and readapted for a new model. We cannot live or discuss without the help of a vocabulary! Bridgman stated as a principle that each word of the scientific dictionary should correspond to a measurement that could be effected in a laboratory. We discussed this statement, which corresponds to a classical idealization that is almost unrealizable in modern physics. The notion is excellent for all of science, in principle, but it is more and more difficult to apply as one goes deeper and deeper into the infinitely small. We can never see directly the ultimate components of matter, but we imagine them, we try to guess their behavior, and we allot them some strange properties in order to coordinate very mysterious experiments. What are these ultimate components? Are they particles? Are they waves? No definite answer can be given. Our imagination builds up a composite model out of seemingly contradictory parts, and science goes on without ever coming to rest.

5. CONNECTIONS OR OVERLAPPING: CONDITIONS RELATING DIFFERENT THEORETICAL MODELS

When a new theoretical model is invented, it usually overlaps, at least partly, with some of the theories previously utilized. For instance, we may remind the reader of Maxwell's electromagnetism, which overlapped with much of the old elastic theory of light. The nature of this coincidence must be clearly understood:

A. Both theories yield similar relations between the *observable* quantities, those of direct interest to the experimenter.

B. Both theories disagree about *nonobservables*. The elastic theory of light discussed a rigid "ether," with two elastic coefficients λ and μ, assumed to be adjusted in such way as to yield no longitudinal waves, but only transverse waves. Maxwell assumed no elasticity in ether, only a set of electromagnetic equations automatically giving transverse waves. The two representations overlapped very gently in most respects, and an older textbook of optics could be easily translated into Maxwell's optical theory without any trouble. The theory of the rainbow rested on identical equations, except for the names of the quantities appearing in the formulas. Things which did not agree were unobservable quantities in either theory. The name "ether" was still common to both models, and a strange "ether-wind," imagined in the old theory, was maintained without much discussion. This was, however, disproved by the Michelson experiments, and since "experiment is always right," something had to be changed in the basic structure of the electromagnetic model. This was accomplished by Lorentz, and completed by Einstein with relativity.

In addition to a decent theory of light (without quanta), Maxwell's and Einstein's theories did introduce a variety of connections with a great many other fields such as electricity, magnetism, and mechanics. They represented a most spectacular improvement in the organization and *interconnection* (or understanding) of our general knowledge.

The specifications are clear: Different theories must obtain similar relations between observables. They may differ on nonobservables; and the new theory must produce the proof that the points of difference *are not observable*. It was necessary to prove that ether had no elastic properties (how could planets move through a rigid ether?), and that ether's absolute motion did not mean anything (Michelson).

Let us now consider another aspect of this synthesis: It is usually stated that relativistic mechanics reduces to classical mechanics when velocities are small and distances are not too large (see Chapter II, Section 10), and this is perfectly true. However, there is, in classical mechanics, a very large field of applications which have no direct connections with relativistic mechanics: *many-body* problems build up the most important part of classical mechanism, and they are often impossible to state in relativistic terms. This is a matter not only of mathematical difficulty, but also of a lack of fundamental assumptions.

So, a great part of classical mechanics cannot be smoothly extended into relativity, at least for the time being.

Classical mechanics is not entirely absorbed into relativity. There is a good deal of overlapping, but not a complete fusion.

This exemplifies our statement that theories have to be considered as very useful models, but nothing definite. They are *human inventions*, not divine revelations; they will be changed, modified, adapted, readjusted, etc., etc., *ad infinitum*, as long as scientists keep working.

REFERENCES

Brillouin, L. (1962). "Science and Information Theory," 2nd ed., Chapter 20, p. 289. Academic Press New York.

Chapter V

THE OPINIONS OF PLANCK, BOHR, AND SCHRÖDINGER

1. BEWARE OF "ISMS"

A strange sickness has been spreading during the past century, progressively paralyzing independent thinking: It might be called the folly of "isms." People seem to be afraid of standing alone: they dare not utter a personal opinion; they must stick together, belong to a disciplined group, follow a leader carrying a banner with a single word "... ism." This kind of insanity was especially dangerous in art, and a painter had to belong to one school or another, such as impressionism, cubism, futurism, non-objectivism, etc. Whether this disciplined uniformity was of help to the artist, remains very doubtful.

In the philosophy of science, a very similar tendency is easily recognized, with the banners of positivism, realism, idealism, determinism, and material-ism. The corresponding theories may have been useful, at one time, by giving a vivid formulation to some vague, general ideas which needed clarification, but which, even if they contained a certain amount of validity, were very wrong in pretending to represent the whole truth! Philosophical theories about science are on just the same level as any other scientific theory: they have a limited domain of application, and a limited accuracy. No thinker should ever pretend to foresee the future.

A philosopher of the 19th century had some knowledge of classical physics, and could watch the first discoveries in electricity and magnetism. On this limited basis he could build a theory, but no one would ever have thought of the incredible changes to appear in our 20th century, with relativity, quantum theory, etc. These new discoveries forced upon us a very painful reappraisal. We have to discard many old chapters of the former scientific philosophies, and things will have to be fitted together differently. Instead of using an old theory and trying to revitalize it with a "neo" prefix (neo-positivism, for instance), it may be safer to start all over again from the beginning, and to scrutinize carefully the present situation and its logical foundations.

Furthermore, let us be careful not to indulge in wishful thinking: we may examine and discuss the science of today, in order to state its methods and present logic, but we are unable to build the philosophy of science for the 21st century, since we have no idea of what science will look like in the year 2000. Scientific theories are based on observations, and represent logical structures for interconnecting experimental facts. Philosophical theories about science are based on the observation of scientific facts and theories. In both problems, a certain amount of extrapolation can be attempted, but certainly will fail if carried too far. Imagination has to be used in all theories, but it must be checked by observation, and the actual facts always have the final word.

We do not intend to discuss the various "isms" of philosophical theories of science. Most of them, for all their value, belong to the past. Old theories are a fascinating field for the investigations of historians, and much can be learned from their partial successes or failures. This century, however, has brought forth an incredible revolution in science. It has been as important, for scientific thinking, as the renaissance was in art. It is now time to examine and scrutinize this fantastic accumulation of new data, and such a task must be done with an open mind, free of old prejudices.

Some famous scientists attempted this difficult discussion. We will try to summarize their very important remarks.

2. Max Planck's Criticism of Positivism

The importance of Max Planck's lectures, pamphlets, and books on the philosophy of science cannot be overestimated. The man who shattered the very foundations of classical physics was, by character, a resolute builder. He would not leave behind him some battered ruins, but he wanted to re-build, starting from the foundations, and his papers are really fundamental. We shall attempt to summarize his viewpoint and we choose to follow one of his most important pamphlets (M. Planck, 1931).

Knowledge stems from our own perceptions and sensations which constitute the substance of our thinking. A narrow positivism intended to limit each individual to the knowledge of his own sensations: Other human beings, around him, appeared to him only as ghosts, hard to distinguish from the phantasies of his imagination. To use an image to which we shall come back later, each individual considered himself as the sole spectator of a comedy, played on the stage by all the other human beings, with the outside world, alive or inanimate, as scenery. Such a limitation really appears as much too arbitrary, and cannot be reasonably maintained. Even an animal is quick to recognize the importance of other animals around it: sight, hearing, yells, beatings, and petting convince him fast enough. Man communicates with his neighbors through more complex and refined means: language and writing. His motto is not only, "I think and I am," but also "I see, I hear, and I speak; I read and I write; I live in a society." The narrow positivist, mentioned above, contradicts himself as soon as he speaks, writes, and seeks to convince individuals around him, while he pretends to treat them as ghosts.

In order to stress the change of point of view, we specify that, hereinafter, each individual has no right to consider himself as a unique spectator of the comedy. The other men are spectators as worthy as he. The whole of humanity is in the audience and speaks, gossips, and discusses the show. On the stage, we may imagine the outside world: animals, plants, and the inanimate world (as long as we discuss physical sciences).

It is imperative to take into account, from the beginning (and in so doing, we deviate from the order of discussion followed by Planck), the capacity for exchange of observations, ideas, and theories through language. The exchange of ideas cannot be ignored for a moment, for, without it we would have neither philosophy nor science. Speech distinguishes man from animals; superior apes do not possess, in their brains, the so-called speech center, and their capacity for thought is thereby heavily reduced. Science and philosophy could never exist without language and libraries.

3. Science Based on Experience

Science wants to be human, not individual. It is made of a network of knowledge, valid for all humanity, and collectively accumulated. In this, it is different from art, which is an individual creation; the artist can live and develop by himself. Van Gogh and Gauguin were completely ignored while alive; they had really created in absolute isolation. The scientist cooperates in the building of a collective monument, to which he contributes a few stones and some concrete. What Sadi Carnot had not been able to finish was rediscovered later by Clausius, Kelvin, and Boltzmann. Quite on the contrary, what has not been expressed by an artist will never be found again: Schubert's "Unfinished Symphony" remains unfinished; as does the "Adoration of the Magi," by Leonardo da Vinci, in the Uffizzi Museum of Florence. (Fortunately, no "restorator" has yet touched it, daring to butcher it as so many other museum pieces—alas!)

Science is built on the ensemble of perceptions gathered and noted by man, and it strives to summarize them in a résumé of general value.

Such is the basis of Planck's discussions.

Relying upon empirical laws and looking for connections among the facts, science does not risk any contradiction: two observations correctly made cannot logically be contradictory. Moreover, we try our best not to ignore whatever can be observed.

Difficulties start as soon as the scientist leaves this solid ground and intends to describe the objects or the world by themselves, such as he imagines them to go on existing, even at times when no observation is actually made. Any absolute statement relating to the properties of the world around us must be considered as an unjustified extrapolation. Only a description based on observations and *relative* to the process of observation can be valid. Many examples might be selected: Ptolemy or Copernicus are both right, since only the relative motion of the earth and the sun can be measured; but Copernicus's hypothesis, supposing that the sun is at rest, allows for a simpler description. Many accounts of astronomy are very far from empirical facts, and are based on analogies or comparisons; strictly speaking they might be called scientific poetry. In fact, these theories are very useful to coordinate observations, but only these observations should be considered as scientific. Theories may change, as long as they check with facts. All we can say with certainty is that observed facts are connected "as if" such and such a theory were true.

Science, as we were saying, is a collective work, and assembles all the information supplied by experimenters *worthy of our trust*. It is obvious that it is very useful to repeat experiments every time it is practically feasible. This is all the more necessary since some experiments yield only laws of probability, and a single experiment, in this case, is without great value.

Upon these fundamental data, carefully controlled, is built the work of theoreticians, looking for logical relations among facts, establishing laws, and attempting predictions.

4. The Outside World and Physical Representation of the World

In this thinking process, it has been admitted for centuries (since the Greek philosophers, Schrödinger tells us) that the scientist could consider himself as an observer isolated from the rest of the world, looking around him without touching anything, and playing the role of an inert witness, enclosed in a glass cage. This conception of an objective world was soon proved as unacceptable in biology or in psychology; in the science of life, one rapidly recognizes the fact that any observation perturbs the object under observation, and that the outside world is unable to keep an unchanged objective structure, when we attempt to observe it too closely.

Similar remarks have recently affected physics, where it was found impossible to maintain the idea of an imperturbable, objective world. Old classical physics admitted the possibility of measures causing no perturbation; we have recently been brought to recognize the fact that there always is a perturbation, especially if we look for high precision. This point is of the highest importance and will require special discussion later.

As far as the inert physical world is concerned, Planck suggests the following position:

A. There exists an outside world, independent of us;

B. This world is not directly accessible to us;

C. We imagine simplified models which serve us as *physical representations* of this inaccessible world.

Definitions A and B are somewhat metaphysical; what is the use of speaking of an inaccessible world? This surpasses our understanding. These postulates have, however, a real importance, through the sharp distinction which they introduce between a natural outside world and the physical representation which we imagine.

This distinction is subtle; it is difficult to express it clearly. It is in the nature of things that we should have trouble conceiving a world to which we have no direct access but that is nevertheless real, surrounding us. It is however essential that we get used to the idea that this outside world, against which we bump at every turn, cannot be completely and objectively defined by our experiments. However, these experiments are the only means of knowledge at our disposal. The rest is poetry, imagination. The attitude taken by Planck appears here in full light: our sensations and our experiments are the only elements which really count. These empirical data present regularities; we can note in them some definite laws. To express these facts, scientists had imagined an objective outside world, unalterable and independent of us. This conception added to our initial perceptions plenty of new ideas, imaginings, which could be of some momentary use, and help us to express ourselves. Actually, these added notions belonged to the domain of fiction. Nothing was forcing on us the idea of an objective and unalterable world, which existed only in our dreams.

Let us come back to the three fundamental assumptions quoted above. Planck himself notes the apparent opposition between statements A and B, and he explains that there is no way to avoid an irrational element in science. We must face the fact that science will never be able completely to fulfill its mission, and give us a definitive and final description of the outside world. This situation must be fully understood and included in the basic statements of a true philosophy of science.

The specification of a scientific theory as a "model" or representation of the physical world (*physikalisches Weltbild*) is a very important philosophical statement, especially when it comes from an outstanding scientist like Planck. He explains very clearly the personal role played by the scientist who starts a new theory: he must have a broad knowledge of the problems of science, and also a vivid imagination. We emphasized in previous chapters the role of imagination and the essential point that theory is "nature visualized by man"; a certain part of the theory is inspired by observation but another part is man's own invention. As Planck states it: theory contains a definite amount of arbitrary notions (*Willkur*). A certain hypothesis, invented by a scientist, may be a partial failure, but some other assumption may lead to a very powerful line of research: this explains why science does not progress steadfastly, in a monotonous and regular way; on the contrary, it proceeds by successive explosions, jumping to the right or to the left in a sort of random walk, and each new successful hypothesis starts a surprising eruption, with unpredictable discoveries. Then, after a while, it reaches its domain of usefulness, stops at more and more road blocks, until a brand new method is invented. In order to emphasize the personal role of the theoretician, Planck speaks of his full sovereignty in proposing a new hypothesis that may lead to a completely new model; the only conditions are lack of internal contradictions, correct overlapping with previous models, and useful predictions. However, the scientist should never confuse the actual outside world with his *self-invented physical world model*. He is happy and proud to understand fully all the properties of his model, but this does not mean that he actually knows much about the outside world around him. It is also essential to keep in mind the fact that every observation perturbs the outside world, since it requires a coupling between observer (and his equipment) and the part of the world under observation. We shall come back later to this most essential remark, when we discuss the work of Bohr and Heisenberg.

Planck's discussions are really inspiring, the style is clear, the thinking is brilliant and unprejudiced, the ideas are supported by a great variety of examples. Read it yourself, and you will find it both profitable and enjoyable.

5. SCHRÖDINGER AND THE GREEK INHERITANCE

Schrödinger was also intrigued by the problems of the philosophical background of science. He discussed it in many lectures and papers. Let us especially quote two very interesting pamphlets (Schrödinger, 1954, 1958).

Trying to summarize the debate, Schrödinger presents, in somewhat different form, the fundamental postulates, and this is what he suggests:

"A. *Principle of understandability of nature*. Appearances of nature can be understood. We must give up invoking miracles or magic. Let us try to specify what we mean by "understood."

"B. *Principle of objectivation*. We observe, in our experiments and our sensations, regularities, successions that can be reproduced. . . .

"C. . . . for which we seek simplified, economical descriptions, cutting out useless details through the use of representations or models."

Thus presented, Schrödinger's remarks offer a rather striking parallel with Planck's.

Then follows the classical hypothesis with which we are all obsessed: the passive spectator observing what goes on among the actors on the stage. The scientist (outside subject) looks at the object, admittedly unchanged, untouchable, unalterable under his look. This picture of an objective real world around us is what we have inherited from the Greeks, and we must get rid of it through surgery of the mind, however cruel it may be. This is where, in our opinion, it is not possible to accept Schrödinger's viewpoint, which is too restrictive nowadays.

We cannot abstract ourselves from the world. We form, together with it, an unseparable whole. There are no actors and spectators, but a mixed crowd. The modern scientist must absolutely renounce the idea of a real objective world. What science does is to supply us with representative models capable of imitating regularities (or laws) which we observe, and to enable us to reason about them. The models constitute the physical representation of the world, such as defined by Planck. *Physical models are as different from the world as a geographical map is from the surface of the earth.*

It had been recognized long ago that an observation required some sort of interaction between the observer and the observed element; but it was currently assumed that this interaction could be made very small and negligible. For instance, looking at the object under observation was supposed to cause no trouble! Quantum theory has completely modified the situation. The finite quantum of action h discovered by Planck makes it impossible to go to the limit of infinitely small action. When you look at an object, you can see it only if you receive at least a few quanta, $h\nu$, from it. The *interaction is finite*; the coupling between observer and observed object cannot be ignored. *It is impossible to make any observation without perturbing the object.*

Schrödinger's first and second principle are worded in a slightly dangerous way. "Understanding" has a different meaning for each reader. Schrödinger takes it in a rather limited and restricted way; "understandable" means for him, "according to human logic"; and he states: "The uncertainty principle, the alleged lack of causal connection in nature, may represent a step away from this first principle, a partial abandonment."

There seems to be no reason to restrict freedom of thinking and to assume old prejudices to be true forever; Planck's point of view is much broader and more general: we observe some regularities in our experiments, and we formulate empirical laws that will later be connected together by some theoretical models.

The model need not be that of an objective immovable world around us; philosophers of our time cannot ignore the fact that interaction between observer and observed is finite and cannot be made as small as desired. Observation and perturbation inevitably go together, and the world around us is in a perpetual flux, because we observe it.

Whether we like or not, these are the facts resulting from Bohr's and Heisenberg's famous discussions.

6. Bohr's Complementarity

Planck's viewpoint and Schrödinger's statement are very close, especially if the words "understandability" or "objectivity" are taken with a rather broad meaning, and are not supposed to imply the existence of an outside world that might be observed without any perturbation.

Accepting this common statement as a reasonable point of departure, we may now discuss problems relating to quantum physics and examine the positions of N. Bohr, W. Heisenberg, and M. Born.

Bohr (1958) explains a number of examples of his theory of *complementarity* that plays a prominent role in quantum theories. Let us, for instance, consider a variety of experiments about the properties of light: some of the observations strongly suggest the idea of light particles, and seem to support the old Newtonian corpuscular theory; but many other experiments can only be interpreted by means of propagating waves. These descriptions seem to contradict each other, but, according to Bohr, they must be considered as *complementary*. Each kind of experiment excludes the other, and they cannot be performed at the same time. Each of them contains only part of the truth. Let us restate here our opinion that a physical theory is nothing but a special model of the outside world—a representation of the physical world, according to Planck.

We are faced with two distinct models: the corpuscular theory and the wave theory. The standard representations of particles and waves that we use are based on usual human experience, and correspond to a variety of observations made in large-scale experiments. These large-scale models do not fit exactly with submicroscopic problems. Observations made about light, or electrons, or any other elementary component of matter require both waves and particles, depending upon the type of experiment performed.

We may introduce a comparison: let us take a snapshot of a landscape using an infrared screening filter; then, we take another picture with an ultraviolet screen. Both pictures will have much in common, but they also exhibit strong differences. We may call them complementary, and the actual situation is rather similar to the one described by Bohr. The "complementary" double image underlines one aspect or the other of a reality which our language, and our images, cannot describe fully.

Complementarity entails a corollary: *uncertainty* (in Heisenberg's meaning). The example of quantum physics can explain this relation. Let us examine an electron in motion: it may pass through a narrow opening in a diaphragm; its position can then be rather accurately defined, and the experiment leads to the image of a particle in motion. However, this experiment and this representation, which constitute the first aspect of complementarity, cannot be followed up with extreme precision. On the other hand (second complementary aspect), we can observe interference effects and thus measure a wavelength λ. This defines a momentum p related to the wave length λ by the relation

$$p = \frac{h}{\lambda} \quad \text{(L. de Broglie)} \tag{V.1}$$

and leads to a wave representation. These two categories of experiments limit and exclude each other. Both cannot be conducted at once with absolute precision. That is what is specified in Heisenberg's principle of uncertainty, which determines the border line between the two methods, and makes sure that complementarity cannot turn into contradiction.

The whole situation of complementarity actually represents a very curious case of "the overlapping of two models," as we called it in Chapter IV, Section 5.

The corpuscular model and the wave model have more points in common than was previously imagined. Thanks to the finite value of Planck's constant h, the quantized particle and the quantized wave yield similar values for energy and for momentum; a "wave packet," as defined by Schrödinger, is located in a certain limited region that corresponds to the "position" of the particle. If we try to define this position too exactly, the momentum can no longer be measured with great accuracy; the error Δx of position, and the error Δp_x of momentum, are related by Heisenberg's uncertainty relation

$$\Delta x \, \Delta p_x \geq h \tag{V.2}$$

In other words, the quantized particle has many physical properties that make it very different from a large-size particle (say, a billiard ball); the quantized wave, too, is very different from a sound wave or a wave on the sea. Both models have many points in common, and overlap nicely, but neither of them can be easily visualized, and the border between both models is defined by condition (V.2).

7. Incomplete Models, Complementarity and Uncertainty

These problems are of foremost importance, and we may be excused for discussing them again and again. The value of science is in question, as well as the confidence we can have in scientific results.

In the preceding section, we outlined the notion of complementarity, so dear to Niels Bohr. If at first glance this idea might sound too subtle, we can now understand its deep logic. The models which we invent in order to classify our empirical results cannot be pure inventions, for our mind does not possess so creative a power. Our models are based on our usual experience, on a human scale. We start by imagining a three-dimensional space, just like the one of the room in which we write, with its floor and its walls. How could we build a box of that type on an atomic scale? We cannot answer the question, but we have no other model available! So we are engaged, from the start, on too restricted an hypothesis: we want to describe the virgin forest, and we imagine it in a cage, as at the zoo.

The strange thing is that, with so poor means, and so prosaic an imagination, we manage to formulate workable models—partially workable at least. Clever as we are at ball games and ballistics, we imagine elementary particles everywhere around us and we discuss their collisions or their capture. These naive pictures already can solve many problems. However, there is another kind of experiment which recalls the properties of waves: interferences, diffraction, etc. We then try the wave model, and our attempt is not without success. Nevertheless, how can we reconcile these two representations which seem to contradict each other?

If we study them more closely, we discover many similarities between particles and waves. Energy and momentum can be defined in a similar manner. The spin of particles and the polarization of waves have many characteristics in common. If we do not take either model too strictly, they can support each other without unsettling each other; they are *complementary representations* (after Bohr).

Furthermore, when we say that neither model can be taken literally, we do not talk idly: the conditions of uncertainty (or of indeterminism) of Heisenberg show, very exactly, the boundary not to be trespassed. As long as we do not pass this border line there is no contradiction, and the two pictures complete each other harmoniously.

The story which we have just outlined is already very old. The light theories have fluctuated, since Huyghens and Newton, between waves and corpuscles. Finally, we must have both ideas at once, and Planck's constant serves as a border line between the domains of application.

Heisenberg's uncertainty principle prevents any actual contradiction. At the same time, and reciprocally, Bohr's complementarity is needed in any discussion of uncertainty. This can be shown by a very simple example, and a careful examination of all examples produced would show a similar procedure (Bohr, 1958; Brillouin, 1956 or 1962, Chapter 16). Let us assume that we want to use a diaphragm in order to determine an area through which a beam of light is transmitted. If we assume the light to consist of *particles*, a beam of light would be similar to a jet of water or to a spray of bullets from a machine gun. In this model, each bullet has a certain momentum p, and there is no connection between the error Δx of the position, and the error Δp of the momentum. This would correspond to a classical mechanical model.

Yes, but: at this point, we switch to the wave model and we discuss the behavior of a wave with a wavelength λ, using Eq. (V.1) of L. de Broglie to connect p and λ. Hence we use *waves instead of particles, and* we specify a quantum connection between these two representations.

This is where we implicitly introduce Bohr's idea of complementarity. When this bold step has been taken, it becomes a simple matter to note that a wave λ passing through a diaphragm Δx is *perturbed*. Diffraction of the wave is inevitable, and this scattering means a change Δp in the momentum p (here we come back to the original corpuscular representation).

All other examples involve similar reasoning, switching from particles to waves, and specifying quantum rules so that our quantized particles are very different from the old-fashioned particles. Furthermore, quantized waves do not look at all like standard mechanical waves, but these new particles and waves are perfectly matched together.

All this results in a finite interaction (defined by the finite h value) between the observed beam of light and the piece of apparatus (diaphragm) used for the experimental observation. We had already emphasized this interaction (or perturbation) in Section 5.

In all this discussion we intentionally left out the role played by probability laws; this will be discussed later.

Complementarity, uncertainty, and *perturbation*—this is what our present quantum theory has to offer. Yet the theory has achieved tremendous success; furthermore, all attempts to build up a "more logical" interpretation have ended in complete failure, at least up to now!

Shall we accept this strange double-faced model as a definitive law of nature, or simply as a temporary unfinished piece of theory? There is no scientific answer to such a question. It is a matter of creed, or wishful thinking. The quantum theory is the best we have at present. Nobody knows what may happen to it in the future. *However, one thing is certain:* experimental facts that have been interconnected or related through quantum theory will have to remain interconnected and related. Planck's constant h has been measured in a fantastic variety of experimental observations, and is thus on solid ground. The quantum is here to stay, even if theories may undergo many changes.

REFERENCES

Bohr, N. (1958). "Atomic Physics and Human Knowledge." Wiley, New York.
Brillouin, L. (1956). "Science and Information Theory," 1st ed. Academic Press, New York.
Brillouin, L. (1962). "Science and Information Theory," 2nd ed. Academic Press, New York.
Planck, M. (1931). "Positivismus und reale Aussenwelt." Akad. Verlag. Leipzig.
Planck, M. (1932). "Where is Science Going?" 221 pp., see especially Chapters II and III. Norton, New York.
Planck, M. (1936). "The Philosophy of Physics," 125 pp. Norton, New York.

Planck, M. (1949). "Scientific Autobiography & Other Papers," 187 pp. Philosophical Library, New York.

Planck, M. (1960). "A Survey of Physical Theory," 117 pp. Dover, New York.

Schrödinger, I. (1954). "Nature and the Greeks," Chapter VII. Cambridge Univ. Press, London and New York.

Schrödinger, I. (1958). "Mind and Matter," Chapter III. Cambridge Univ. Press, London and New York.

Chapter VI

THE ARROW OF TIME

1. Is Time Reversible or Not?

Everybody knows that time can never be turned back, and that the past will never come again. The man in the street knows it, and the poets lament it; this is one of the severest hindrances of our life.

Many physicists, especially those interested in thermodynamics, were deeply impressed by the impossibility of reversing the course of time, and by the correlation with the continuous increase of entropy in an isolated system. Let us quote a very remarkable statement by Lord Kelvin:

If Nature Could Run Backward[1]

> If, then, the motion of every particle of matter in the universe were precisely reversed at any instant, the course of nature would be simply reversed forever after. The bursting bubble of foam at the foot of a waterfall would reunite and descend into the water; the thermal motions would reconcentrate their energy and throw the mass up the fall in drops reforming into a close column of ascending water. Heat which had been generated by the friction of solids and dissipated by conduction, and radiation with absorption, would come again to the place of contact and throw the moving body back against the force to which it had previously yielded. Boulders would recover from the mud the materials required to rebuild them into their previous jagged forms, and would become reunited to the mountain peak from which they had formerly broken away. And if, also, the materialistic hypothesis of life were true, living creatures would grow back-

[1] From Kelvin (1874).

ward, with conscious knowledge of the future but with no memory of the past, and would become again, unborn.

But the real phenomena of life infinitely transcend human science, and speculation regarding consequences of their imagined reversal is utterly unprofitable. Far otherwise, however, is it in respect to the reversal of the motions of matter uninfluenced by life, a very elementary consideration of which leads to the full explanation of the theory of dissipation of energy.

Various illustrations have been given of the vivid description presented by Lord Kelvin. Movie goers have had many opportunities to watch a waterfall climbing up the hill or a diver jumping back on the springboard; but, as a rule, cameramen have been afraid of showing life going backward, and such reels would certainly not be authorized by censors!

In any event, it is a very strange coincidence that life and the second principle should represent the two most important examples of the impossibility of time's running backward.

How does it happen that some scientists take the opposite point of view, and try to convince us of time's reversibility? This merits discussion, and the falsity of these scientists' opinions must be clearly pointed out.

Most of these men are more influenced by mathematical theories than by experimental observation. They believe in their theoretical models more than they care about actual facts. The first example may be found in classical mechanics: equations of motion, established by Newton, do not involve the sign of time. If a bullet moves on a certain trajectory from north to south, another similar bullet might move along the same trajectory from south to north. Let us immediately point out that the statement can be *correct only if* all damping terms happen to be zero. They should be exactly zero, not just negligible!

Air resistance is one of these damping terms, or, if we consider electric charges, damping due to electromagnetic radiation is unavoidable. *Physics does not know any motion without damping:* The moon is moving around the earth, and it provokes tides in the oceans; these tides dissipate a large amount of energy, and the motion of the moon is damped. The calculation is classical, and the resulting damping is not negligible.

So, the point of departure of the discussion of time reversibility is wrong, and corresponds to an unrealistic oversimplification. This is the type of error a mathematician is able to make, and classical mechanics has been unduly abandoned to pure mathematicians for centuries.

Even if we agree to discuss a mechanical system without damping, the preceding problem is not correctly stated. Equations of motion are reversible, truly enough, but they represent only part of the actual story. They are no more than the stage setting, the place where the comedy is going to be played.

The real play starts when actors come in. The actors, in mechanical problems, may be represented by particles, and by rigid bodies. Their initial positions and velocities must be defined; with these initial data, and the equations of motion, we finally have a real problem.

Here again, mathematicians manage to evade the correct question; they speak of *given initial conditions*, as if this was a secondary matter. However, it is not! At the risk of repeating what was already explained in previous chapters, *initial conditions are never given* (except in examination problems); they result from a careful study of the past history of the whole system.

When an astronomer wants to compute the motions in the solar system, he starts with a discussion of all observations made during previous centuries; from these experimental data he computes the positions and velocities of the planets, comets, satellites, etc. at a certain date, and these initial data are known within certain limits of accuracy. When this is done, the computation of motions in the future can be performed, if the computer is equipped with a reliable electronic computer.

Here we recognize the common situation: *the past commands the future.* Accurate knowledge of the past may enable us to make reliable predictions, but these predictions will become hazier and hazier when the computation is carried further and further into the distant future, and finally we have to stop, because we know that our predictions have no practical value!

Even if we assume all damping mechanisms to be naught, we must recognize the fact that initial (or final) data are not reversible: Firing a gun in a non-reversible initial condition and receiving a bullet in the head is a very much nonreversible final result.

We shall examine mechanical theories more carefully in the last chapters of this book, and we will discover a number of very weak points in classical mechanics. A great theorem of H. Poincaré summarizes clearly conditions where rational mechanics is unable to yield definite practical results; and these situations are very many, although usually ignored in standard textbooks.

2. The Role Played by Time in Problems of Wave Propagation

We may easily recognize, in the problem of wave motions, a situation very similar to conditions discovered in the preceding section. Wave propagation equations are insensitive to the sign of time. Waves may propagate to the right or to the left. As a matter of fact, it is well known that wave equations obtain two sorts of solutions: retarded waves or advanced waves. Retarded waves are the ones which we always use in physical problems: they are emitted from a source and spread away from it. The farther away they go, the later they arrive. Advanced waves would propagate toward the "source," and if they come from far away, they would have been started in the distant past.

Here we can immediately recognize that the problem of the *time arrow* is not a problem of propagation equations: it is a problem of *boundary* conditions. The "source" is on the boundary; nothing can be started within the propagating medium itself.

What Do We Call a Source?

Mathematicians certainly are in trouble when it comes to defining a source of light, or of sound, etc., in general terms. They also are in trouble when defining an ideal absorbing medium. Most physical problems of diffraction assume an "absorbing screen" with no reflection. It has a very practical physical meaning, although it does not correspond to any simple boundary condition. Sommerfeld spent a great deal of time trying to set up suitable mathematical conditions for the representation of an "absorbing surface," and he had to invent some very ingenious (if not absolutely convincing) devices. Lord Rayleigh met with similar difficulties in acoustical problems.

An experimenter working with optical systems *starts* with the notion of a source of light, as distinct from an object illuminated by the light. He cannot do the simplest experiment if he does not realize, very precisely, the meaning of these words. This is true for large scale experiments, and it remains indispensable at the atomic or subatomic scale. The source of light (emitter) falls from a high energy level to a low energy level. The absorber gains some energy, and is raised to a higher energy level. *Reversing the arrow of time* would interchange emitter and receiver, and it would *turn the energy scale upside down*. This is obviously too much!

Equations of wave propagation are symmetric with respect to time. *Boundary conditions are not symmetric* in time.

Once these physical boundaries are set, then sources, reflecting surfaces, and absorbers are practically defined (although the mathematicians often do not know how to do so), and we *must use only retarded waves*, starting from the sources and finally absorbed in the receiver.

The problems we met in this section are rather similar to those encountered in classical mechanics, but for the difference that light velocity is finite, and that, according to Einstein, no action can be transmitted at infinite velocities. On the contrary, Newton assumed all forces to act at finite distances in an infinitely small time. This was indispensable for the proof of his third law, of equal action and reaction!

What happens to actions and reactions with finite velocities of propagation is quite a problem! For electromagnetic fields, Maxwell had to invent a very ingenious system of "Maxwell's tensions," and the problem seemed to be solved. However, we now have many new waves (or new particles) in wave mechanics, but nobody has yet tried to define tensions in the "space" where these waves are propagated. But this, as Kipling would say, is a different story, and it may not be told today.

3. General Remarks about Retarded Waves

Why should we use retarded waves, and why not advanced waves? In a nutshell: just because retarded waves yield the correct answer. Advanced waves have been used by many theoreticians, and they never checked with experimental facts.

It seems that we might attempt to state some general remarks, corresponding to present scientific knowledge:

A. Physical laws should make use of effects transmitted by waves; electromagnetic waves for light, Dirac waves for electrons, and more and more ψ waves for new particles recently discovered.

Instantaneous transmission at finite distances appears nonphysical.

B. All our laws enable us to predict the future (at least for some time) on the basis of a correct observation of the past. We *cannot observe the future* before it happens, and this makes *retrodiction impossible.*

C. It has become customary to speak of "given initial conditions" at a certain time t, including given velocities, accelerations, etc. This oversimplification may have been useful in classical mechanics; it is certainly not sufficient for a prediction of the future in physics. Knowledge of the distant past, of all waves *en route* to our domain of observation, is required; it cannot be replaced by "initial conditions" at a single instant of time, even if they include higher time derivatives.

D. *Time reversal is not allowed.* Emission and absorption are not symmetrical. The laws and probabilities for emission and absorption are different.

E. *Classical mechanics* and classical electromagnetism represent only *approximative visualizations* of actual facts. Their laws may be symmetrical in time, but they have to be completed by dissymmetrical boundary conditions. It is not surprising that these laws, completed by boundary conditions, and by our remarks A–D, result in irreversible time, thermodynamics and statistics.

Time is not reversible, although some special areas of physics may be insensitive to the sign-of-time arrow.

4. Short Historical Survey; the Ritz–Einstein Discussion

These fundamental problems were discussed on many occasions. Let us quote some notable instances of particular importance.

Albert Einstein (1909) and W. Ritz (1908, 1909) published, separately and together (Ritz and Einstein, 1909), some very interesting papers in which two different questions were discussed:

A. Theory of blackbody radiation;

B. Use of retarded and/or advanced potentials for electromagnetic waves.

On problem A, the paper of Einstein is a historic one. He had previously introduced (Einstein, 1905) the idea of "light quanta" or bullets $h\nu$ traveling with a velocity c, that we now call *photons*. In the 1909 paper, he rediscussed the problem of energy fluctuations in blackbody radiation, and proved that Planck's radiation formula led directly to a fluctuation formula requiring the existence of photons. The method used in this old paper has been reproduced in many textbooks, as, for instance, the present author's book on information theory (Brillouin, 1956 and 1962a, Chapter 9, p. 126).

Problem B raised a lively discussion. Einstein took the position that advanced or retarded waves were only mathematical tools to be used for discovering an actual solution of any special wave problem. Ritz emphasized the viewpoint that retarded waves were the only ones that may have physical significance; no advanced waves can be experimentally observed. Ritz saw clearly that this was the direct result of *boundary conditions*, although in many instances the fact may be obscured by the arbitrary simplification of assuming the boundary at infinite distance. Conditions at infinity are very often forgotten or left unclearly specified. Also, *initial conditions* of the whole system are responsible for the special role played by retarded waves. Ritz seems to have been the first one to state this point of view, which we have more explicitly developed in preceding sections.

In a few words: Ritz states that time is essentially not reversible, that an experimenter knows and observes only retarded waves, propagating from source to observer, from emitter to receiver; that these facts must be added to the general theory of wave propagation; and that there is no difficulty in so doing, because these conditions are contained in the boundary conditions. Any wave equation must be completed by boundary conditions, if you want to obtain a real problem; and experimental boundaries always satisfy the relations imposing retarded waves.

5. PAST, FUTURE AND RELATIVITY

The theory of relativity raised many discussions about "past," "future," and "simultaneity," and it is interesting to show that the new relativistic definitions agree completely with the viewpoint presented above. Let us draw a diagram (Fig. 5) with the distance

$$r = \pm(x^2 + y^2 + z^2)^{1/2}$$

as abscissa and ct (c, light velocity, and t, time) as ordinate; according to Einstein's first theory of relativity, no signal can propagate faster than c. A signal emitted from A ($r_A = -3$, $ct_A = -6$) and moving forward with velocity c is represented by a ray Aa at inclination $\pi/4$. If another signal propagates more slowly, it may give a ray like Aa′. A signal emitted from A_1 and propagating backward with velocity c will reach $r = 0$ at a_1.

On our diagram, we must distinguish these different regions:

The *past* is a conical region about negative t values, characterized by the fact that any phenomenon occurring at points A or A_1 may send a signal reaching $r = 0$ before $t = 0$. It may thus influence point 0 ($r_0 = 0$, $ct_0 = 0$).

The *future* is a conical region about positive t values. It is the ensemble of all points that may be influenced by something happening at point 0.

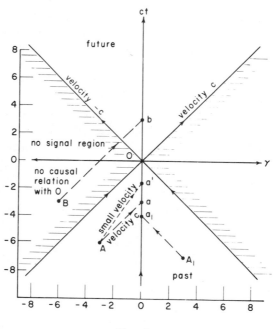

FIG. 5.

A *no man's land*, or better said, a *no signals region* (hatchings on Fig. 5), extends between past and future. A point B from this region is unable to influence 0. A signal from B propagating with velocity c will reach $r = 0$ at a point b in the future. It may act at $r = 0$ only after time t_b, and cannot have any effect at 0.

The past can influence 0; the future can be influenced by 0; but the no signals region has no causal connection with 0. It ignores 0, and is ignored by 0.

Old classical mechanics assumed an absolute time that corresponded to the idea that actions could be propagated at any distance instantaneously (meaning infinite velocity). In these old theories, there could not be any "no signals' region"; past and future were in contact all along the plane $t = 0$.

What is new in Einstein's theory of relativity is the complete separation between past and future, with the strange "no signals region" sandwiched in between; and this situation makes our viewpoint even easier to adopt. Of course, Einstein assumed time-symmetry in his theories, but this assumption was superimposed and not needed. It simply does not play any role, because of the complete distinction between past and future.

6. RECENT DISCUSSIONS ABOUT TIME IRREVERSIBILITY

The assumption of time reversibility was stubbornly maintained by most mathematicians and theoreticians, none of whom seemed to introduce any new ideas into the discussion. The matter came again into the open in recent years with papers by J. A. Wheeler and R. P. Feynman (1945), S. Watanabé (1955), and the brilliant discussions of O. Costa de Beauregard (1958, 1962, 1963), who emphasized the impossibility of blind retrodiction, which he calls "Bayes' principle." A short summary of the debate was presented by L. Brillouin and L. Rosenfeld (1962) at the end of a meeting of the *Académie Internationale de Philosophie des Sciences*.

We followed their general arguments at the beginning of the present chapter, and we may add a few words as a conclusion: Time never went backwards, and we can safely assume it never will. We may walk back and forth, left and right, or up and down. Space components wear no arrow and x, y, z are reversible. This is not true for time, according to century-old, human knowledge. Propagation equations, for all sorts of waves (light, matter, and corpuscles of any kind) are reversible, but boundary conditions, containing the detailed circumstances of emission, deflection, and absorption, are not reversible. At the end of the discussion, L. Rosenfeld quoted the point of view of the Copenhagen School and said:

> All your statements are indisputable. According to indications given by Bohr, I would consider the finite velocity of signal propagation as the real origin of time's arrow. *By definition*, we state that *receiving* a signal from the outside world is *posterior to the emission* of said signal. I am very happy of our agreement on this viewpoint, which is essentially distinct from the usual idea that the arrow of time should be justified by statistical thermodynamics. . . .

The definition thus agreed upon refers to the most fundamental conditions of experimental observations. It applies to elementary atomic or subatomic reactions, while thermodynamical irreversibility rules only macrophysical phenomena.

Reversing time today on the earth is impossible. The reversing process should have been started centuries ago on distant stars, in order to reverse, *now*, the signals we receive from them and the physical actions they have on our local world. Such a reversal would change all the Döppler effects on light, and reverse the red shift into a blue shift. All this is simply unthinkable.

7. CAUSALITY OR FINALITY: BERGSON, FANTAPPIÉ, ARCIDIACONO, AND ELSASSER

In order to remain on stable ground, we were very cautious to discuss, up to now, only physical or chemical problems. We did not attempt to formulate rules relating to life and biology.

We may now look into these delicate questions, and we will try to summarize briefly some recent exchanges of ideas on biological problems. Philosophers, scientists, and laymen have had many opportunities to think about the strange behavior of living beings (especially thinking beings). An overwhelming majority concluded for "finality," assuming that a living being has been built for a special purpose, that it acts with a certain aim. Most thinkers seem to claim that causality may be the rule for inert matter, while life is always aiming for a goal. Without going back to ancient philosophy, we may start with H. Bergson (1908), whose book *"L'évolution créatrice"* marks a date in scientific philosophy:

> No definite category of thought is able to check exactly with the problems of life (Introduction, p. VI). In vain do we attempt to force life in anyone of our frames. The frames are broken. They are too stiff, too tight for what we want to put into them.

And Bergson specifies that neither causality nor finality can be used to represent life. Both are "ready-made clothes" that do not fit the customer, but the philosopher suggests that one of these garments might be readjusted, retailored and some alterations made, in order to fit a little bit better. Thus he proposes to abandon strict finality and to build a new theory of "creative evolution," indicating a tendency to create new creatures of more and more complicated structures, better adapted to life's problems:

> Life cannot reverse the direction of physical processes (pp. 246–247) that is determined by Carnot's principle. However, life acts as a force that (if abandoned to itself) would work in the opposite direction. Unable to stop the motion of matter in its transformations, it is nevertheless capable of slowing it down.

This tendency to create more and more complex structures is an attenuated statement of finality.

The problem was discussed by L. Fantappié, who introduced the idea that finality could be obtained by the use of advanced waves. It certainly is a very striking suggestion, and one which should be kept in mind for further discussion. However, here comes a delicate question: what sort of waves are we going to consider in this respect? Light waves seem out of question. They propagate very fast, while progress in biological evolution is extremely slow.

It seems really difficult to make light waves responsible for biology. This however should not be taken as a negative answer. In modern physics, almost everything is represented by waves, and maybe we shall discover later on that some sort of wave may play also a dominant role in biology. For the moment, the question remains open.

Fantappié's suggestions retained the attention of G. and S. Arcidiacono (1961), two brothers, a mathematician and a biologist, whose book certainly makes very interesting reading. Many interesting discussions are brought forward, and the reader will find in the book much valuable information and much worthy of quotation.

In conclusion, let us recommend the remarkable discussion of W. Elsasser (1958), which represents a masterpiece of analysis and constructive re-appraisal. The author is not trying to lure us into accepting a simplified system of explanation; his aim is to compare physics and biology, and to emphasize all the complexities of the latter. Using cybernetics, information theory, and the theory of perturbation by observations, he tries to obtain a better understanding of the actual difficulties inherent in any theory of biology. His idea of *biotonic laws* is brilliantly presented. This is really an epoch-making essay.

8. TIME ARROW AND CAUSALITY

We shall discuss causality in the next chapter; let us, however, explain right away the direct connection between time arrow and causality. If we have no time arrow, we cannot speak of causality. The rule is that the "cause" takes place *before* the "effect" can be observed. The delay may be extremely small, but it is necessary. If two things happen together, we may discuss a cross-correlation between them, but we cannot tell which one is the cause and which one is the effect. The *delay*, on the other hand, cannot be defined unless the arrow of time is specified. Moreover, very often the delay will be due to the time required for the propagation of a wave from "cause" to "effect."

All problems discussed in the next chapter presuppose agreement on the direction of time. Let us add some more examples:

A. Radioactive disintegration can be used to define the time arrow. Radium always emits its radiation as time goes on.

B. Dating of old specimens by the carbon method assumes a definite time arrow.

C. All the discussions of cloud chamber or bubble chamber tracks are based upon some knowledge of where the incident beam comes from. *Boundary conditions* contain the location of the source of the initial beam. This is a typical example of what we said before.

D. Let us consider a moving electric charge; its acceleration results in emission of electromagnetic waves. Here, *only retarded fields* are to be taken into account, in order to obtain a correct check with experiments.

E. Schrödinger's or Dirac's wave equations contain $(\delta/\delta t)$ (or its equivalent: the energy E), while classical mechanical formulas contain $(\delta^2/\delta t^2)$. This means that classical mechanics (*without damping* or *radiation*) is reversible in time, but wave mechanics is irreversible, just as diffusion and heat conduction are irreversible.

Time dissymmetry is the general rule, although it may not appear everywhere. Remember Curie's fundamental remarks on symmetry: in a dissymmetrical crystal, many properties may exhibit more symmetry than the crystal itself, the complete dissymmetry may not appear everywhere, *but* nothing can be more dissymmetrical than the basic crystal structure itself.

We have a similar situation for time's dissymmetry: it may not appear everywhere, *but* one single example of time's dissymmetry is sufficient to prove the rule.

REFERENCES

Arcidiacono, G., and Arcidiacono, S. (1961). "Spazio Tempo Universo." Fuoco, Rome.
Bergson, H. (1908). "L'Evolution créatrice." F. Alcan, Paris.
Brillouin, L. (1956). "Science and Information Theory," 1st ed. Academic Press, New York.
Brillouin, L. (1962a). "Science and Information Theory," 2nd ed. Academic Press, New York.
Brillouin, L. (1962b). Transformations et Avatars de la notion de champ. *Rev. Métaphys. Morale No.* **2**, 206.
Brillouin, L., and Rosenfeld, L. (1962). Note complémentaire. *Rev. Métaphys. Morale No.* **2**, 247.
Costa de Beauregard, O. (1958). Equivalence entre les deux principes des actions retardées et de l'entropie croissante. *Cahiers Phys.* **96**, 317–326.
Costa de Beauregard, O. (1962). Relation intime entre le principe de Bayes, le principe de Carnot et le principe de retardation des ondes quantifiées. *Rev. Métaphys. Morale No.* **2**, 214.
Costa de Beauregard, O. (1963). "Le second principe et la science du temps." Seuil, Paris.
Einstein, A. (1905). *Ann. Phys.* [4] **17**, 133–138.
Einstein, A. (1909). Zum gegenwärtigen Stand des Strahlungsproblems. *Physik. Z. No.* **6**, 10. Jahrgang, p. 185.
Elsasser, W. (1958). "The Physical Foundation of Biology." Pergamon Press, New York.
Fantappié, L. (1944). "Principi di une teoria unitaria. . . ." Humanitas Nova, Rome.
Fantappié, L. (1955). "Il finalismo originato dalle Scienze esatte." Sansoni, Rome.
Fantappié, L. (1960). "Memoria Postuma," Collectanea Matematica, Barcellona.
Fantappié, L. (1961). "Nuove Vie della Scienza." Sansoni, Rome.
Kelvin, William Thompson, Lord (1874). *Proc. Roy. Soc. Edinburgh* **8**, 325–331. Quoted in "The Autobiography of Science," (F. R. Moulton and J. J. Shifferes, eds.), p. 468. New York, 1945).
Ritz, W. (1908). Über die Grundlagen der Elektrodynamik und die Theorie der schwarzen Strahlung. *Physik. Z. No.* **25**, 9. Jahrgang. p. 903.
Ritz, W. (1909). Zum gegenwärtigen Stand des Strahlungsproblems. *Physik. Z. No.* **7**, 10. Jahrgang, p. 324.
Ritz, W., and Einstein, A. (1909). Zum gegenwärtigen Stand des Strahlungsproblems. *Physik. Z. No.* **9**, 10. Jahrgang, p. 323.
Watanabé, S. (1955). *Rev. Modern Phys.* **27**, 179.
Wheeler, J. A., and Feynman, R. P. (1945). *Rev. Modern Phys.* **17**, 157.

Chapter VII

CAUSALITY AND DETERMINISM; EMPIRICAL LIMITATIONS

1. STRICT DETERMINISM OR LOOSE CAUSALITY?

Science assumes a rule of causality in the world around us. It takes the view that a certain cause will be followed by certain effects. This point of view was, in the past, pushed to the extreme, and exaggerated in the form of a more definite statement: a certain cause must be followed by a certain effect. We intend to show, through many well-known examples, that such *strict determinism cannot be accepted*, because it runs contrary to experiments.

What we actually observe is a loose connection, with extenuating circumstances represented by some rule of *probabilities*. A certain effect E may occur without any visible cause, in which case it has a probability $P_{0,E}$. If a certain cause C is previously observed, then the probability of the effect E is modified, and becomes $P_{C,E}$. The cause C may increase or decrease the probability of the effect:

$$\text{If} \quad P_{C,E} > P_{0,E} \quad \text{the cause has a positive action} \qquad \text{(VII.1)}$$
$$\text{If} \quad P_{C,E} < P_{0,E} \quad \text{the cause has a negative action}$$

Furthermore, we very often observe a *delay* in the action of the cause. If the cause acts at time $t = 0$, the effect may be observed at any later time t and the probability $P_{C,E}$ will depend upon the delay t in the observation.

All these circumstances are contrary to the old-fashioned, strict statement of determinism.

Determinism assumes a "must": the cause must produce such and such effect (and very often one adds, "right away"!).

Causality accepts a statement with a "may": a certain cause may produce such and such effects, with certain probabilities and certain delays.

The distinction is very important. A law of strict determinism may be based on (or contradicted by) one single experiment: the effect is present or it is not. It is a "yes or no" answer, and contains just *one bit of information.* Such a situation may be found occasionally, but it remains very exceptional.

A probabilistic causality requires a very large number of experiments, before the law of probability, as a function of delay t, can be approximately stated. The amount of information contained in such a law would require very precise analysis and some computation. Methods and formulas for this computation were given in another book (Brillouin, 1956, 1962). Instead of strict determinism, we obtain a *law of correlation,* a much subtler type of definition, that may apply to a great variety of problems.

2. A Very Simple Example: Radioactivity

Let us observe a radioactive sample and measure its radiation as a function of time. If the sample is fairly active, we obtain an exponential decay, such as the one plotted in Fig. 6. If we select a poor sample, with little radio-

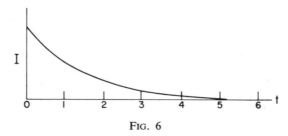

Fig. 6

activity, we may get a curve of the type drawn in Fig. 7, with an average exponential decay, and noticeable up and down fluctuations. This already suggests that the pleasant exponential of Fig. 6 represents only the average of some probability law. In order to investigate more precisely the behavior of

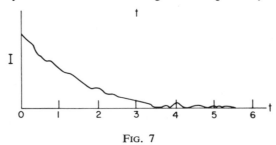

Fig. 7

the elementary processes, we select an extremely poor sample, and observe its radiation with a very sensitive Geiger counter, having itself a very short time constant. With such equipment we record a set of separate pulses, similar to those plotted in Fig. 8. The individual pulses have approximately the same height, but they are more numerous at the beginning, and their spacing increases progressively with time. The higher radiation observed at the beginning, in Figs. 6 and 7, was due to a greater accumulation of pulses, which our recording device was unable to distinguish.

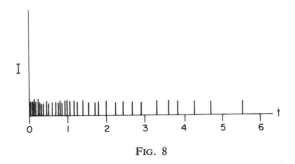

FIG. 8

Altogether, the elementary law of probability is of the following type:

$$\overline{\Delta N} = A \, N(t)\Delta t \qquad\qquad \text{(VII.2)}$$

The radioactive sample contains at time t a number $N(t)$ of atoms ready to undergo a radioactive transformation. During a small interval of time Δt, the number of atoms exploding $\overline{\Delta N}$ is represented, in the average, by Eq. (VII.2). This means that each individual atom has a probability $A \, \Delta t$ of exploding during Δt. We are unable to say *which atom* is going to explode, nor can we say exactly how many atoms may explode. This is a typical law of probability, with all its characteristic uncertainties. Only the statistical rules of the game are known. We summarize the result by giving the *probability P_e* of radioactive transformation for a single atom, per unit of time.

$$P_e = A \qquad\qquad \text{(VII.3)}$$

3. Emission of Light by Atoms

We encounter a very similar situation in the problem of light emission by excited atoms. Let us assume atoms with a ground energy level E_0, and an upper level E_1. When an atom is raised to energy E_1, it may fall back to the ground level E_0 and *emit* radiation ν_1

$$h\nu_1 = E_1 - E_0 \qquad\qquad \text{(VII.4)}$$

Conversely, if the atom rests at its ground level E_0 and absorbs radiation ν_1, it will reach the upper level E_1. Let us call $\rho_1 dv_1$ the energy density in the incident radiation for the frequency interval $\nu_1, \nu_1 + dv_1$. This means that ρ_1 represents the energy density of the radiation field per unit frequency interval.

This density ρ_1 is directly proportional to the intensity of the incident light (Einstein, 1917; Kemble, 1937; Brillouin, 1931).

We are going to discuss the statistics of absorption and emission, according to Einstein (1917). This represents an extension of the problem of the preceding section, and the point of departure of a general theory of emission and absorption of radiations.

The formulas suggested by Einstein, and very successfully checked by experiments, were the following:

Probability for emission of a photon $P_{1 \to 0} = A + B\rho$ (VII.5)
$h\nu$ per excited atom at E_1

Probability for absorption of a photon $P_{0 \to 1} = B\rho$ (VII.6)
$h\nu$ per atom at ground level E_0

with the relation

$$\frac{A}{B} = \frac{8\pi h\nu^3}{c^3}$$

where c is the velocity of light, and h is Planck's constant. If no incident radiation is present, we note that formula (VII.5) reduces to the formula (VII.3) of the preceding section. When, however, there is incident radiation of density ρ, we may have absorption (VII.6) when the atom rests at its ground level E_0, or, on the contrary, exaggerated emission (VII.5) if the atom is at the upper level E_1. These coefficients A and B of Einstein are famous in the theory of radiation. We do not intend to discuss here the very ingenious theory developed by Einstein, nor its very important consequences; great scientists like Ehrenfest, Pauli, Schrödinger and others worked out many theoretical applications of Einstein's formula. The reader may find them discussed in a book of Brillouin (1931).

Experimental checks are very numerous, and of greatest physical importance. The famous invention of Masers and Lasers [Microwave (or Light) Amplification by Stimulated Emission of Radiation] by C. H. Townes is based essentially on the use of the $B\rho$ term of "provoked or stimulated emission" introduced by Einstein.

4. PHILOSOPHICAL SIGNIFICANCE OF EINSTEIN'S FORMULAS

We want to remind the reader of these very well-known facts, because they have much significance in connection with the general problem of causality *versus* determinism.

There is *no strict determinism* in Einstein's formulas. Emission or absorption of radiation cannot be exactly predicted. The elementary processes are only known statistically, in the average. If we have, at a certain moment, N atoms of a radioactive product, we may say that the chance is $A\Delta t$ for any one of these atoms to explode during an interval of time Δt. We have no indication whatsoever about the exact time when a certain atom will actually explode.

Statistics, probabilities, and averages—these are all we know from Einstein's relations, and the situation is exactly similar for absorption and emission of radiation of any kind. We discussed emission or absorption for light, but similar rules apply (with some modifications) to all problems of radiation, collisions, etc.

It is necessary to emphasize these fundamental facts because too many scientists still remain under the impression that all elementary laws should be similar to those of classical mechanics that are supposed to be strictly deterministic. This is not the case. Elementary physical laws are all expressed by statistical formulas. No exact prediction is possible (at least, for the present time) and everything is irreversible! Let us note that Einstein's set of rules corresponds exactly to the statements given in Chapter VI about the irreversibility of time:

A. Emission and absorption are part of the boundary conditions, and are not contained in the wave propagation equations.

B. They are completely irreversible, since we have absolutely no knowledge of individual laws, and we only know average statistical results.

(Right from the start, we are dealing with irreversibility, and this situation directly yields the two following important results)

C. Time is irreversible, in accord with the general discussion of Chapter VI.

D. Entropy is constantly increasing, as was proven by Ehrenfest, Pauli, and others, in direct applications of Einstein's formulas (Brillouin, 1931). Quantum statistics is entirely based on Einstein's laws for emission and absorption of radiation, and their generalization from particles of the Bose-Einstein group to those belonging to the Fermi–Dirac family.

5. QUANTIZED WAVES DO NOT SUPPORT DETERMINISM

For many scientists, it required an agonizing reappraisal to abandon determinism. This philosophy had been the basis of scientific research for centuries. The fantastic success of classical mechanics had made determinism the creed of almost all scientists, despite its difficulties and obvious exaggerations.

First of all, we must emphasize that, contrary to common opinion, *classical mechanics is not exactly deterministic*; this fact results directly from a famous theorem of Poincaré, and the matter is of such importance, that we shall devote three chapters to the discussion of these delicate questions in the second part of the present book.

What we now want to examine carefully is the fact that there is *no escape from uncertainty in quantum mechanics*, and that this uncertainty is very directly *supported by direct experimental evidence*.

When Schrödinger formulated wave mechanics and introduced his ψ functions, he was certainly prompted by a desire to restore determinism in quantum problems. Moreover, he was hoping that waves instead of particles would be the only change required, and might cure all the troubles and uncertainties of quantum theories. A similar opinion was supported by L. de Broglie, who took a slightly subtler viewpoint when he proposed "guided particles" following the trajectories selected by the "pilot waves." This general line of reasoning was strongly emphasized by the Russian school, especially by V. Fock, who wrote and lectured about determinism reinstated through wave theory, and claimed to have convinced N. Bohr. Here, the desire is obviously to maintain strict obedience to Marx and Hegel, who took determinism for granted. What should we think of these viewpoints? Are they reasonable or untenable? The answer must be carefully worded, and the problem will be split into two distinct sections:

A. If the ψ waves of Schrödinger were exactly similar to *classical* waves, they would define a new determinism, different from the determinism of particles in classical mechanics. Acoustical waves are just a special chapter of mechanics; their laws were very exactly derived from mechanical theorems by Lord Rayleigh, and there is no uncertainty in them. The change from particles to waves would be, in this case, exactly similar to the change from geometrical optics (based on Newton's corpuscular theory of light) to the so-called physical optics based on wave theory by Fresnel and Young. This is obviously the reasoning in the back of the minds of the supporters of wave-theory determinism. The equations of L. de Broglie and Schrödinger differ seriously from the standard wave equations of mechanics, but nevertheless they look deterministic in their behavior.

B. *Yes but!* Quantum waves of a *classical type do not suffice*; they represent the first step, and must be completed by a second step, that is definitely non-deterministic. We shall explain this second problem in two different ways, which complete the description of the quantized world (at least as it appears at present—and nobody can predict the future evolution of scientific theories).

We thus distinguish two successive viewpoints:

B.1. *Max Born's statistical connection* between waves and particles;

B.2. Methods of "*second quantization*," also called superquantization, that change the character of the waves, and introduce discontinuities in the waves themselves, thus giving them properties very similar to those of quantized particles.

We already emphasized in Chapter V, Section 7, the fact that our quantized particles enjoyed all sorts of special properties that make them very different from the standard particles of mechanics. We also noticed that quantized waves had only some vague similarity to standard waves; and we stated that these new waves and new particles represented the two complementary aspects of matter, according to N. Bohr's complementarity.

It is now time to specify more clearly what we meant by these general statements.

6. BORN'S STATISTICAL INTERPRETATION OF WAVES

Truly enough, Schrödinger's waves follow a differential equation very similar (although not identical) to standard wave equations, but the wave equation does not tell the whole story. We must investigate the *conditions of observation*, the *boundary conditions*, and the circumstances under which waves may be emitted or absorbed. We encounter, here again, a problem similar to the one discussed in Chapter VI. Physically, all boundary conditions, or initial conditions, are of the upmost importance.

When we dealt with usual physical waves (waves on the sea or acoustical waves, for instance), we could always easily observe and measure the amplitude (call it ψ) of the wave at any point, and also the phase of the wave. A great variety of optical devices could be used and would provide accurate experimental methods for these purposes.

There is no way—*absolutely no experimental way*—of measuring the amplitude ψ of a Schrödinger wave. Amplitude and phase cannot be observed. The only quantity that can be measured is $|\psi|^2$, the intensity of the wave, and we shall see in a moment how indirectly we observe it.

Whenever we attempt to observe a ψ wave, we absorb it, and it suddenly changes its character. We were looking for a continuous wave and we get discrete particles.

If we observe a light beam, it disintegrates into photons (light quanta) of energy $h\nu$, that raise some atoms from their ground level to a higher energy level. If we experiment with a ψ beam, we obtain electrons or other particles, and so on. The wave breaks up to pieces, and these pieces are connected with the wave in a strange fashion.

The photons have an energy $h\nu$, that depends only on frequency ν, and has no connection with the energy of the light beam. The energy (or intensity) of the beam is related to the number of photons falling on the receiver during each second. The size of the photons is always $h\nu$, whether the beam is very intense or incredibly weak!

The situation is similar with Schrödinger waves. The wave is related to certain types of particles (electrons for instance) and the intensity $|\psi|^2$ defines the *number of electrons* per second striking the target.

This is *Born's statistical law:* The average intensity $|\psi|^2$ of the wave yields the average number of particles per second. At what definite time does a particle strike? We do not know. Only the average number is defined and nothing more. Here we *lose any kind of determinism*!

Standard mechanical waves were deterministic, and could be observed in all details. Schrödinger's waves are invisible, and yield only some statistical information about certain types of particles.

When we observe the ψ waves and the light waves, the deterministic character suddenly slips through our fingers.

We may show, by a simple comparison, how much these quantum waves actually differ from usual waves. Let us assume for a moment that waves on the sea follow quantum laws: very long and powerful waves, having very low frequency, would have small quanta $h\nu$; each such quantum would be practically unable to do any damage to a sea wall. On the contrary small ripples of much higher frequency would exhibit large $h\nu$, and be able to destroy the sea wall by throwing all its stones away!

7. SUPERQUANTIZATION

Here we wonder: "Has it any meaning to speak of such elusive waves? Are they really waves? Or what else may they be?"

More precisely: is it reasonable to assume continuous waves of the usual standard type, when we only observe discrete particles? The discontinuous character cannot appear suddenly at the moment of observation. The "wave" is emitted by quanta; it is absorbed by quanta. We should try to maintain this quantized character during the propagation!

This was done by the method known as "second quantization" or "superquantization," and it worked in a very satisfactory way, getting rid of many of the inconsistencies of the wave–particle dualism.

The method was generalized by Pauli and Heisenberg for electromagnetic fields, and these authors obtained quantized electromagnetic waves that could be interpreted either as waves or as photons. Thus, the dual character was introduced, right from the beginning, into the fundamental equations, and Bohr's complementarity was given a solid mathematical formulation.

In this short description, we intentionally omitted a number of details, and even many important points. One thing, however, should be mentioned especially: there are at least two different types of "particles," namely, fermions (ruled by Fermi–Dirac statistics) and bosons (with Bose–Einstein statistics). For the corresponding waves, the distinction rests upon Pauli's exclusion principle: a single ψ wave may carry any number of bosons, but if we deal with fermions, there can be only one of them on each single wave; a single wave is defined as a proper solution with given boundary conditions, and with a specified spin component. Photons are of the boson type, electrons and protons are fermions, and other particles belong to bosons, if their spin is integral, or to fermions when they have half-integer spins. Superquantization describes the number of particles guided by a certain wave. It is obvious that the superquantization will follow different rules for fermions and bosons; it is a very striking new character of this quantization that it introduces this systematic distinction clearly.

We might start here developing the modern aspects of quantum theory, and discuss the properties of all the "elementary" particles recently discovered, but this would be beyond the program of this book.

8. Transformations and Metamorphosis of the Idea of Fields

Field of gravitation, electromagnetic field—we are always using the same word, "field," but we have traveled very far from the original field idea of Faraday. The word itself seems to come from a rather candid visualization: a sort of lawn, where the ground would represent the "space," and the grass growing on it might correspond to the force vectors available at each point in the field. There was obviously the assumption that the vectors were already available there, before we actually did observe or measure them.

The field of gravitation was assumed to exist before Newton's apple happened to allow him to see it. In a classic electromagnetic field, we took the field for granted; it was supposed to be defined by the charge, currents, and magnets "creating the field," even before we introduced any measuring device (that might perturb the original field!), or before we happened to send through this field a beam of electrons, whose trajectories would reveal the field.

The field had acquired for the physicists a strange property of material existence. Scientists and engineers used to speak of a *given field*, and forgot to explain how the field had come into existence, and what sort of equipment was producing it. This, however, was based on some curious assumptions that were not clearly specified: the field acted on electrons, but the reaction of electrons on the field was ignored. This was reasonable if a heavy piece of apparatus was producing the field, getting the reaction from the electrons but remaining practically unperturbed by this reaction.

Think of gravity: an apple falls in the gravitational field of the earth. The earth pulls the apple down but the apple pulls the earth up! Of course we ignore the motion of the earth, but what about principles?

There was (and there still is) absolute belief in the conservation of energy and momentum. How could these "principles" be reconciled with field equations? A moving electron emits an electromagnetic field that may act upon a second electron. Both have the same weight. The second electron reacts on the field that transmits the reaction back to the first particle. This delicate problem was very carefully discussed by Maxwell, who invented a system of "tensions," a tensor being built up of products of the field components. Maxwell's tensions get the impact from moving electrons and transmit it all around; they accompany the electromagnetic waves and balance the mechanical effects of the fields. This represents a very elegant solution of the problem: electromagnetic fields and their tensions accumulate and transmit both energy and momentum.

The practical use of these general formulas is often very intricate, but they represent a perfect theoretical solution. The theory of relativity started from Maxwell's equations, and was later generalized to include gravitation. Instead of being instantaneously created at any distance (as was assumed in Newton's mechanics), gravitation is supposed to propagate with a finite velocity. One should then find, for these gravity waves, another system of tensions, similar to Maxwell's tensions and capable of transmitting both impulse and energy. These tensions must be derived from the modified, non-Euclidian geometry of Einstein. Corresponding formulas can be computed, together with many details about gravitation waves.

This again is a very consistent answer to the problem of conservation for energy and momentum in the wave. These formulas may be checked experimentally and verified by the observation of radiation pressures.

Radiation pressure was first discovered by Lord Rayleigh for acoustic waves. It can be computed (Brillouin, 1938, 1963) by averaging the elastic tensions in the medium transmitting the acoustic wave, during the propagation.

In a similar way, radiation pressure for electromagnetic waves is computed from the averaged Maxwell's tensions in the electromagnetic field of the waves. The method is general and can be applied to any kind of classical mechanical or electromagnetic waves.

What is the situation with the waves of *wave mechanics*? This is another example of the fact that these waves do not at all resemble standard mechanical waves. Nobody ever computed "tensions" for the ψ *waves*; it was never assumed that these waves were real enough to transmit momentum or energy. This was the job of *particles guided by the waves:* photons, electrons, etc. Instead of computing tensions, physicists attempted to clarify the correlation between waves and particles, and these attempts culminated in the theory of quantized electromagnetism of Pauli and Heisenberg. In these schemes, Energy and Momentum conservation should come out as statistical laws.

This theory was briefly discussed in Section 7; let us only add that its fundamental assumptions were very ingeniously justified by Bohr and Rosenfeld, who managed to reduce the definitions of quantized electromagnetism to some direct discussions of the experimental conditions of measurability.

The situation looked brilliant, and the success of the theory was highly praised in theoreticians' circles, but, alas, some unexpected difficulties suddenly appeared: a variety of integrals were nonconvergent, and led to infinite values. Many attempts were made to avoid these roadblocks, but without success; it was obvious that the troubles were related to the use of infinitely small lengths (or wavelengths), but nobody could discover a remedy, and in a lecture before the American Physical Society, R. Oppenheimer conceded that the theory was "a monumental flop."

One of the most troublesome of these divergent integrals was the total energy of a particle, that should yield the mass (mc^2), and could not be computed.

Such pessimism, however, was not actually justified. A way out of trouble was very ingeniously suggested by Schwinger (1958) and it is known under the name of "mass-renormalization." This very important method deserves a few words of explanation, since it has opened new ways for theoretical investigation with most remarkable predictions.

Let us rapidly sum up this step, which started with the discoveries of Lamb and Retherford. These authors demonstrated (1947) that the fine structure of the second level of hydrogen did not correspond to Dirac's predictions: the level $2S$ should (according to Dirac) coincide with the level $2P\frac{1}{2}$, but is, however, about 1000 megacycles higher. After many unfruitful attempts, one explanation was advanced by Hans Bethe.

This author notes a strange gap in Dirac's system of equations: the increase in mass corresponding to kinetic energy is correctly included, but no increase in mass is foreseen to correspond to the electron potential energy in the electric field. Dirac's theory is therefore obviously incomplete, and can satisfy the relativistic condition only in the absence of an outside field.

Bethe, having noticed this important gap, remedied it by approximations, and computed a correction of 1040 megacycles. Such a brilliant result drew the attention of other scientists, and Schwinger grappled with the whole problem. The difficulty was to evaluate the mass resulting from a divergent integral! Schwinger avoided the actual calculation (in fact, impossible), but he managed to eliminate the original mass, by comparing the formulas for the electron at rest and in motion, and by eliminating from the two problems the same infinite integral, relativistically transformed. He still was unable to remove the divergent integral of mass, but he brushed it aside and made it harmless. It may be called patchwork, but the patching is really artistically woven.

He thus obtained a correction in the mass caused by the potential energy in the field, and was able to re-introduce this forgotten term in the wonted place. This method received the name of "renormalization" of the mass. The explanation given above is very crude. It is only meant to outline the general direction of the computation. The practical results are excellent, and the calculations check in a great number of examples. Nevertheless, the basis is not very solid, and we cannot clearly formulate the fundamental hypotheses, nor the essential definitions of such a theory.

A complete theory will have to take into account all the interactions among all the "elementary" particles, whether stable or unstable. Well, there are too many particles already, and new ones are discovered every day. As long as a final list of these intruders has not been established, and a general theory to classify and coordinate them has not been invented, it does not seem possible to establish a total theory of all these fields and their interactions.

Let us try to measure the distance traveled within one century: our fore-fathers had one elastic ether, propagating optical waves; we now pretend to have no ether (Einstein blew it up!), but we use some thirty different equations for the waves of that many "guided particles," and nobody knows how to organize this incredible crowd of formulas. There is still plenty to do for our children and grandchildren. Let us wish them good luck!

9. SOME EXAMPLES OF OVERLAPPING THEORETICAL MODELS

The very brief summary that was presented here draws only the main lines of the history of quantum physics. It was intended to show the successive changes, adaptations, and modifications of theoretical models. Many points were taken for granted in the first sketches, and had to be revised or radically modified later on. This meant that, at each step, there was a great deal of overlapping with preceding models, and the following question arose: How much of the previous theory did we keep unchanged, and where did we retouch and correct the preceding statements?

Such questions required careful investigation. Let us select some examples that retained the attention of the present author:

A. The *B.W.K. method* has become classical; it specifies the relations between wave mechanics and the first quantum theory of Bohr and Sommer-feld, which started from classical mechanics. This old method was based on the classical Hamilton–Jacobi procedure, completed by some quantum conditions. It looked completely different from wave theory, but it was found possible to build up a system of successive approximations, starting from Bohr–Sommerfeld (with some minor adjustments) and progressing toward a solution of the wave equations. This was done almost independently in 1926 by L. Brillouin, G. Wentzel, and Kramers; hence the B.W.K. initials. The best presentation and discussion of the method is found in the textbook of E. C. Kemble (1937).

For an English translation of this author's original papers, see L. Brillouin and L. de Broglie (1928).

The method is widely used for practical computation in many problems of quantum chemistry; it had been originally intended as an investigation of the exact conditions of junction between successive theories, and a discussion of the corrections included in wave mechanics. At the same time, it was discovered that classical mechanics and wave mechanics do not overlap too closely. This is clearly visible from the fact that conditions for separation of variables are not the same in both cases; discontinuities in classical solutions do not correspond to discontinuities in the wave problems, and this discussion has never been completely clarified. We shall come back to these enigmas in Chapter X.

B. The *Brillouin theorem* refers to the theory of multi-electronic structures. Here we have two different methods: the first one starts with the general Hamiltonian and the corresponding wave in a multidimensional space. The second method uses a set of individualized functions for each electron, and introduces a "self-consistent field" representing an approximation of the interactions among the different electrons.

The self-consistent field was first proposed by Hartree and greatly improved by V. Fock. It was proven that Fock's solution represented the best possible approximation of the general problem; this result is now quoted everywhere as the "Brillouin theorem," and the original papers are found in two pamphlets: Brillouin (1934) and a paper that Brillouin (1935) read at a meeting in Geneva.

This last paper contains a summary of the different methods of self-consistent fields for electrons in metals. A table (p. 44) gives a detailed comparison of fundamental assumptions, formulas, plots of energy, etc. The following lines summarize the most important results for the Fock–Dirac method:

> Fock–Dirac represents the best possible approximation with separated waves for each electron. The total energy requires a correction for electrostatic interactions and a small exchange correction. These corrections, however, are practically constant and do not modify the *energy differences, which are correctly given.*

This formulation is just the so-called *Brillouin theorem.*

Pauli, who attended the Geneva meeting was actually impressed by this statement and emphasized that it was a very important proof.

Many systems of approximations have been developed in connection with problems of chemical structures and quantum theory. The reader may often be confused by conflicting statements based on incomplete sets of approximations. The discussions published by P.-O. Löwdin (1957) are especially clear. A variety of approximations are now being used in the applications of-wave mechanics. Each of them, separately, may yield good results; but a mixture of different (and often incompatible) approximations is bound to be wrong, because some corrections will be counted twice, some other corrections may be used in problems where they do not apply, and finally some absolutely necessary corrections (too difficult to guess) will simply be ignored. Beware of "semi-empirical" methods, which Löwdin very carefully puts apart in a separate category.

C. *The Brillouin zones.* Electrons in metals or semiconductors are represented by waves propagating through the whole crystal lattice. These waves can be built in different ways: (1) one may start from solutions obtained for isolated atoms and compute the effect of some coupling between atoms;

(2) we may, on the contrary, use free electrons in the crystal as a point of departure, and compute the perturbation due to fixed ions.

These two methods were difficult to compare; they gave frequency bands that did not seem to have similar structures. The junction between these two methods was made possible by a discussion that introduced the very useful idea of "Brillouin zones" (1953). The importance of this method was hailed by Sommerfeld as a fundamental achievement in the electronic theory of metals. This method is now used in most textbooks and forms the basis of Shockley's theory of semiconductors. The numerical calculations about zones and energy bands were greatly improved by Frank Herman (1954), who was able to make complete numerical computations for a variety of crystals.

REFERENCES

Brillouin, L. (1931). "Quantenstatistik," pp. 177–192. Springer Berlin.
Brillouin, L. (1934). Les champs self-consistents de Hartree et de Fock. *Actualités sci. et ind. No.* **159**, 37 pp.; L'atome de Thomas-Fermi et la méthode du champ self-consistent. *Ibid. No.* **160**, 46 pp.
Brillouin, L. (1935). *Helv. Phys. Acta* **7**, Suppl. II, 33–46.
Brillouin, L. (1938). "Les tenseurs en mécanique et en élasticité." Masson, Paris (2nd ed., 1949).
Brillouin, L. (1953). "Wave Propagation in Periodic Structures." Dover, New York.
Brillouin, L. (1956). "Science and Information Theory," 1st ed. Academic Press, New York.
Brillouin, L. (1962). "Science and Information Theory," 2nd ed. Academic Press, New York.
Brillouin, L. (1963). "Tensors in Mechanics and Elasticity." Academic Press, New York.
Brillouin, L., and de Broglie, L. (1928). "Selected Papers on Wave Mechanics." Blackie, London.
Einstein, A. (1917). *Physik. Z.* **18**, 121.
Herman, F. (1954). Some recent developments in the calculation of crystal energy-bands. New results for the Germanium crystal. *Physica* **20**, 801–812. Amsterdam Conference on Semi-conductors, and many other later articles.
Kemble, E. C. (1937). "Fundamental Principles of Quantum Mechanics." McGraw-Hill, New York. Reprinted by Dover, New York, 1958. p. 449–Chap III, pp. 43, 90, 152, 168, 181, 572.
Löwdin, P.-O. (1957). *J. Phys. Chem.* **61**, 55 and many reports of the ASTIA.
Schwinger, J. (1958). "Quantum Electrodynamics." Dover, New York. (34 selected papers by different authors.)

Part 2

Uncertainty in Classical Mechanics

Chapter VIII

WEAKNESSES AND LIMITATIONS
OF MECHANICS

1. The Need to Scrutinize Classical Mechanics.
What is Space?

For centuries, classical mechanics has been the stronghold of determinism. The siege of this citadel must be laid; reconnaissances have shown the limits of its jurisdiction outside its walls, but there are also strong limitations to the power of determinism within the fortress itself where it seems most solidly entrenched.

Mechanics starts by assuming the existence of *absolute space and time* as defined by mathematicians. This is not even stated, it is simply taken for granted. We discussed the problem of time in Chapter VI, but the definition of space itself is very tricky. We had a word about this problem at the beginning of Chapter III, when we briefly sketched a discussion that was elaborated upon in another book (Brillouin, 1962). Without unnecessary complications, the problem can be summarized in three steps:

A. To measure a length l, we need a ruler with subdivisions of the order of magnitude of l (or smaller).

B. For moderate distances we may use a rigid ruler (a crystal for instance) or a wavelength λ, but for extremely small distances, we have no other choice than a wavelength.

C. This wavelength λ itself is measured by observing its quantum

$$E = h\nu = h\frac{c}{\lambda} \qquad \text{(VIII.1)}$$

D. When the wavelength λ becomes extremely small the quantum $h\nu$ rises to very high values; let us measure it by the corresponding mass m_0, using

85

Einstein's relation

$$E = \frac{hc}{\lambda} = m_0 c^2 \tag{VIII.2}$$

hence

$$m_0 = \frac{h}{c\lambda} \approx 2.2 \times 10^{-37} \lambda^{-1} \tag{VIII.3}$$

When λ becomes really small, the mass m_0 increases beyond all limits. It is thus impossible to define infinitely small distances, and the idea of continuous space (and time) is completely meaningless.

We may add some precision to the preceding summary. The second step, B, was carefully discussed in the book (Brillouin, 1962), with the conclusion that most favorable conditions obtained for

$$\frac{\lambda}{2} = l \tag{VIII.4}$$

Furthermore, it was proven that the type of wave chosen for the experiment was of secondary importance in dealing with extremely small λ and very high frequencies ν, since all waves behave in a similar way at very high frequencies.

Formula (VIII.3) was used for computation in Chapter III, Eq. (III.2), assuming a wavelength of 10^{-50} cm, and that resulted in a fantastic mass of 2×10^7 metric tons. Such an enormous mass would be annihilated in a single operation to create the wavelength λ. This is really unthinkable.

The steps C and D are not sheer imagination. This procedure is the one followed to evaluate the wavelength of cosmic rays.

When a ray of very small wavelength is absorbed in an ionization chamber, it provokes a large bundle or shower of particles ejected in all directions. The energies of these particles are computed separately and added together. Their sum represents the quantum $h\nu$ of the incident radiation.

Formula (VIII.2) is well known. Assuming m_0 to represent the mass of a certain particle (electron, meson, proton, etc.), the formula yields the *Compton wavelength* λ. for the corresponding particle.

Here are some orders of magnitude:

	Particle			
	Electron	Proton	Ne	U
Mass	$m_e \approx 9 \times 10^{-28}$	$m_p \approx 1.7 \times 10^{-24}$	$20\, m_p$	$238\, m_p$
Compton $\lambda = \dfrac{h}{mc} \approx \dfrac{2.2}{m} 10^{-37}$	2.4×10^{-10}	1.3×10^{-13}	0.65×10^{-14}	0.55×10^{-15}

The Compton wavelengths for light atoms are of the order of magnitude of 10^{-13} cm, and it is currently assumed that distances smaller than 10^{-13} cm are almost impossible to measure. The Copenhagen school calls this 10^{-13} cm length a "Femtometer." In order to obtain a wavelength of 10^{-15} it would be necessary to annihilate a uranium atom in a single stroke!

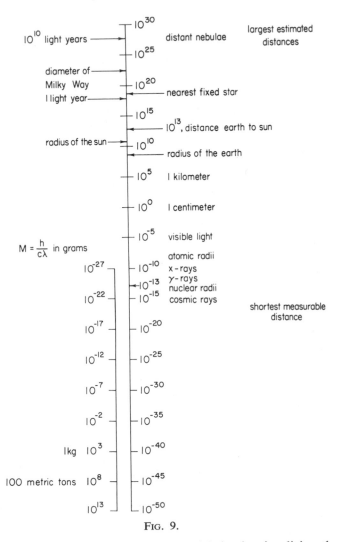

Length in cm. on a Logarithmic Scale

FIG. 9.

Figure 9 explains the whole situation, and helps in visualizing the actual scale of measurable length. At the bottom of the figure, a special scale indicates the corresponding masses m_0 according to Eq. (VIII.3).

2. ERRORS AND INFORMATION IN MECHANICS[1]

The theory of information has obliged the physicist to re-examine the role of experimental errors and has required a complete re-appraisal of their actual importance.

Formerly, errors were usually considered as a secondary effect, a nuisance that could be neglected on most occasions, and which should be ignored by theory. The assumption was that errors could be made as small as might be desired by careful instrumentation, and played no essential part. This was the point of view of mathematicians discussing the axioms of geometry, and most physicists accepted, implicitly or explicitly, this kind of idealization. Modern physics had to get rid of these unrealistic schemes, and to realize the unpleasant fact that errors cannot be made as small as one wishes, but must be taken into account as an integral part of the theory.

Until the end of the nineteenth century, most scientists assumed that experimental observations could reveal the "laws of Nature"; of course, observations were perturbed by all sorts of errors, but it was customary to generalize the imperfect data available and to formulate simple mathematical laws; these *exact* laws were supposed to govern the outside world, whether it could be observed in principle or not. For example, Newton's laws of mechanics and of universal gravitation were accepted as rigorous, even though they had been verified only within the limits of experimental error.

The first difficulties were encountered in connection with statistical thermodynamics: How was it possible to derive irreversible thermodynamics from strictly reversible mechanical laws? There was also the problem of determinism, which was assumed to be proved by scientific investigations, although in practice it remained impossible to verify such a rule by any experimental device.

With Heisenberg's "uncertainty principle," the importance of errors in observations came into the foreground. Physicists realized that it was impossible to measure accurately, and at the same time, a coordinate x and its momentum p_x, and that the corresponding errors were coupled by the relation: $\Delta x \times \Delta p_x \geq h$. Any experiment measuring x with an error Δx perturbs the system and introduces an unknown change Δp_x in p_x, making its exact determination impossible. It is a fundamental and inescapable fact that an observation always creates a perturbation. If you have a physical system which is completely isolated and unperturbed, you cannot observe it. An observation necessarily requires a certain temporary coupling between the system and a measuring instrument; this coupling results in a perturbation of the observed system.

[1] Sections 2 and 3 are revised from a paper of the author published in *Nature* **183**, 501 (1950).

This general remark was given a precise statement in a law called the "negentropy principle of information." It states that an observation yields a certain amount of information ΔI, that this information can be measured quantitatively, and can be compared with an inevitable increase in entropy ΔS in the measuring device during the experimental measurement. The net result is (in entropy units):

$$\Delta S \geq \Delta I \quad \text{or} \quad \Delta I + \Delta N \leq 0 \qquad \text{(VIII.5)}$$
$$\text{with } \Delta N = -\Delta S \quad \text{neg(ative) entropy}$$

These conditions mean that a finite amount of energy ΔE must be degraded and changed into heat:

$$\Delta E = T\Delta S \geq T\Delta I \quad (T, \text{ absolute temperature}) \qquad \text{(VIII.6)}$$

The definition of the quantity ΔI can be summarized in a simple way (Brillouin, 1956, 1962): let P_0 be the number of equally possible cases before the measurement, and P_1 the number of such cases after the observation. Then, by definition:

$$\Delta I = k \ln \frac{P_0}{P_1} \qquad \text{(VIII.7)}$$

where k is Boltzmann's constant. If the accuracy is very high, P_1 becomes very small and the amount of information is very large. Infinite accuracy, with infinitely small error, would mean an infinite increase in information; hence an infinite amount of energy ΔE is degraded, which is quite impossible.

A similar opinion has been expressed by Born (1953, 1955, 1961) in a series of papers based upon the obvious fact that every method of observation has its limitations, making experimental errors unavoidable. This is, in a general way, what is stated more precisely in our condition (VIII.6).

The preceding conditions can be explained in simple terms. It has been realized, since the work of Ising, that Brownian motion (thermal noise) sets a limit to the accuracy of observations. Thermal agitation involves energies of the order of kT per degree of freedom. For a reliable observation of one degree of freedom, an energy larger than kT must be used in order to overcome irregular motions of magnitude kT. If the observation is made on many degrees of freedom, it will require an energy proportional to T; this energy is degraded, and yields an increase of entropy ΔS independent of T. This is practically the mechanism underlying Eq. (VIII.5) and Eq. (VIII.6).

As for condition (VIII.1), a simple numerical computation shows that the energy E, translated into electron volts, corresponds to the many millions of volts required to measure the cross-sections of particles having very small diameters, Δx. This relation is actually applicable to the synchrotrons and other powerful accelerators used for measuring the very small cross-sections encountered in collisions of atomic particles.

To sum up: an observation is an irreversible process, necessarily involving an increase of entropy in the measuring apparatus; the information obtained is paid for in negentropy. As Gabor has commented, "You can never get something for nothing, not even an observation." This remark has far-reaching implications, which will now be discussed.

3. THE OBJECTIVE WORLD AND THE PROBLEM OF DETERMINISM

In a brilliant discussion, Schrödinger (1954) has explained how much we owe to the Greek philosophers, from whom we inherited many fundamental ideas. These concepts have been extremely useful, but we have now reached a point where we must revise them drastically. The scientist used to step back into the role of an external observer, and to assume the existence of "a real, objective world around us," governed by accurate mathematical laws (the laws of Nature), according to which it would proceed unperturbed, whether we observe it or not.

The modern point of view is different: when we are not making any observation, it must be admitted candidly we do not know what is happening; and when we make an observation, we certainly perturb the "outside world," by some coupling between observer and the observed. So the assumption of accurate laws of nature is gratuitous; it is a philosophical creed, but it is not supported by experimental facts. All we can prove is the existence of certain correlations: given the result of a certain experiment, we are able to predict (within certain limits) the possible outcome of a later experiment. This, however, does not require any objective outside world: that is an additional assumption which may provide a convenient model for most large-scale experiments, but the model is definitely wrong at the atomic or subatomic scale.

Bridgman has repeatedly emphasized the danger of introducing into our theories too many unmeasurable quantities. Sooner or later these unobservable concepts will have to be rejected, and this will often mean a very painful reappraisal of actual facts and data.

In many cases, strict causality must be replaced by statistical probabilities; a scientist may or may not believe in determinism. It is a matter of creed, and belongs to metaphysics; physical experiments are unable to prove or to disprove it. This general point of view may be called the "matter-of-fact" point of view.

Conditions stated in Section 2 above show that it is quite impossible to eliminate experimental errors completely. They are not only a practical limitation but also they represent an absolutely unavoidable feature of the experimental method. Laplace invented, more than a century ago, a demon who was supposed to know exactly the positions and velocities of all atoms in the universe, and to compute exactly the future evolution of the whole world.

The present discussion constitutes an exorcism of Laplace's demon. Both the uncertainty principle and the negentropy principle of information make Laplace's scheme of exact determinism completely unrealistic.

In order to measure very accurately the initial positions and velocities of all the atoms in the universe, the demon would need an infinite amount of energy, according to Eq. (VIII.5) and Eq. (VIII.1). The exact determination of initial conditions is thus physically impossible.

The negentropy principle of information had already provided a definite answer to the paradox of Maxwell's demon; it also eliminates Laplace's demon without further discussion. Experimental errors cannot be made as small as one may wish, for they belong to the actual facts of experiment and must be included in the theory.

4. A SIMPLE EXAMPLE FOR THE DISCUSSION OF UNCERTAINTIES IN MECHANICS[1]

The role of errors in mechanics was usually ignored. The citadel of determinism did not allow intruders. But some mathematicians, within the fortress of determinism, did sense the danger. We shall base all the discussions in this chapter on a theorem of *Liouville*, while the next chapter will rest on a famous theory of H. Poincaré. From there on, we accept all the assumptions of classical mechanics, including the (undefendable) absolute time.

Let us consider a ball moving along the x direction between two rigid walls located at $x = \pm l$. The motion seems perfectly determinate but we want to take account of the inevitable errors in measuring the initial conditions: When we throw the ball, we know the point of departure $x = 0$ only within an error Δx and we can define the initial impulse p only within Δp. This simple problem was discussed by Born. He emphasized the fact that, after a time t has elapsed, we know the position of the ball with an error $\Delta x + (t/m)\Delta p$ and this may soon become larger than the distance $2l$ between walls. Henceforth we only can say that the ball is somewhere between these walls, a result which can hardly be called "determinism."

This very same example has been discussed by E. Borel (1925) in his lectures on statistical mechanics, in order to visualize the exact meaning of the famous *Liouville theorem*. If we plot the motion in the x,p-plane (phase extension) this theorem states that the *area* $\Delta x \Delta p$, defined by the initial errors, moves along the trajectory and gets distorted in an unpredictable way, but always *keeps the same area*. Figure 10 explains the general situation: The points of departure cover the initial rectangle "0," but points with a larger p have also a larger velocity $V = p/m$ and move faster along x; hence, after a short time t we obtain the oblique distribution "I," which has obviously the

[1] Sections 4–10 are revised from a paper by the author's in *Inform. & Control* **2**, 45–63 (1959).

same area as "0." Then comes a reflection off the first wall and a reversal of p, which leads to the shapes "II," "III"; a new reflection off the $-l$ wall would bring the Liouville area back into the upper region. During the motion this area gets thinner and thinner, and is broken into many layers, up and down,

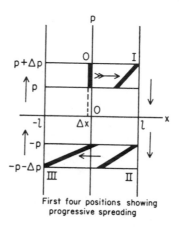

First four positions showing
progressive spreading

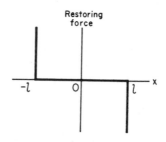

Rigid walls at $x = \pm l$

Fig. 10.

as sketched on Fig. 11. Our experimental techniques cannot be accurate enough to detect all these layers and distinguish between them, and after a while we can only say that the representative points lie within the two rectangles $-l \le x \le +l$ and $p, p + \Delta p$ or $-p, -p - \Delta p$. Furthermore, the average density is uniform in both rectangles. This last result is a form of the ergodic theorem.

It was necessary, for this general proof, to use two fundamental assumptions: (a) Initial conditions are subject to inevitable errors $\Delta x, \Delta p$. (b) Final state is observed with errors $\Delta x, \Delta p$. Both assumptions are direct consequences of the uncertainty principle and of the general conditions of Section 2, if we remember that the amount of energy available in the laboratory (and partly degraded during the measuring experiments) is finite. This limits the entropy increase ΔS to a certain maximum value and makes it impossible to assume infinitely small errors Δx and Δp. The conditions of Section 2 remove any possibility of proving scientifically the validity of

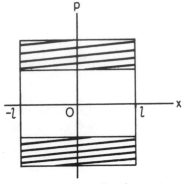

After many reflections

Fig. 11.

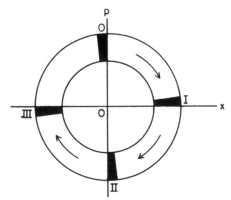

Motion without spreading

Fig. 12.

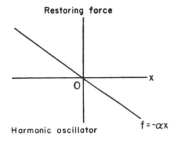

Harmonic oscillator $f = -\alpha x$

determinism. Knowing the initial conditions within certain errors, we can predict the future only for a limited time interval. After that, we do not know exactly what happens. This is the justification for statistical mechanics.

Both the uncertainty principle and the negentropy principle of information make Laplace's scheme completely unrealistic. The problem is an artificial one; it belongs to imaginative poetry, not to experimental science.

5. SOME MORE EXAMPLES: ANHARMONIC OSCILLATORS AND A RECTIFIER

The importance of this subject justifies some more discussion. We start with the harmonic oscillator, where the trajectories in the x,p-plane are ellipses

$$\frac{1}{2m}p^2 + \frac{1}{2}\alpha x^2 = E_{tot} \qquad \text{a constant} \qquad (VIII.8)$$

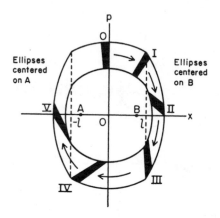

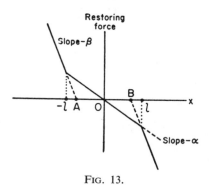

FIG. 13.

A convenient unit change can be used to reduce the ellipses to circles, taking

$$1/m = \alpha$$

Oscillations are isochronous and keep the same frequency for all amplitudes. The result is to maintain constant not only the area but also the shape of the Liouville surface element. This is shown in Fig. 12, where the surface element appears unchanged in positions 0, I, II, and III. There is no spreading of the representative points in this model, which appears as an interesting exception. A similar case will be found for an idealized rectifier shown in Fig. 15.

As soon as the harmonicity is perturbed we see the area spreading again. The case of Fig. 13 corresponds to increased stiffness for large oscillations.

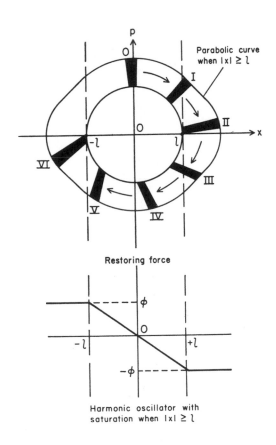

FIG. 14.

The trajectory is an ellipse centered on O for the central part, joining right and left ellipses of centers B and A. On these junctions, the Liouville area takes a position which is oblique with respect to a radius drawn from B (or

A), and this obliquity increases at each revolution. The general situation is similar to that of Fig. 10, and it actually reduces to Fig. 10 if we take $\alpha = 0$ and β infinite.

Another possibility is shown in Fig. 14 with a restoring force reaching the saturation values $\pm\varphi$ when $|x| > l$. The external trajectories are parabolic curves

$$\frac{1}{2m}\, p^2 \pm \varphi x = E \qquad\qquad (VIII.9)$$

and these trajectories exhibit a slow motion. The external points lag behind the inner points. The Liouville area is distorted in the opposite way to that of Fig. 13.

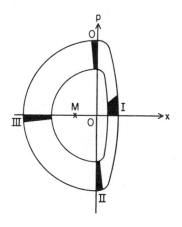

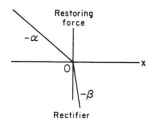

FIG. 15.

Figure 15 corresponds to a sort of *rectifier*, with a weak restoring force $-\alpha x$ on the left and a very strong restoring force $-\beta x$ on the right. The trajectories are ellipses centered on O on both sides and oscillations remain synchronal for all amplitudes. The average center of mass moves progressively to the left when the oscillations become larger and larger, and this represents the rectifying effect. There is no spreading of the Liouville area. Another curious example is represented in Fig. 16 and corresponds to the limit of Fig. 14 when the distance l is zero. The trajectories are parabolic on both sides and the outer part of the Liouville area is strongly lagging behind.

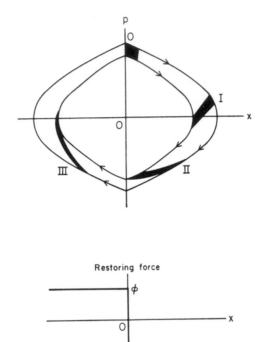

FIG. 16.

6. THE ANOMALY OF THE HARMONIC OSCILLATOR

Looking back at the different examples just discussed, we observe a general situation similar to that obtained in Section 4. The Liouville area maintains a constant value, but it is soon elongated in such a way that it spreads over the whole region of possible motions. There is one exception, represented by the strictly harmonic motion (Fig. 12) or by the more artificial rectifier of Fig. 15. In these two examples the Liouville area maintains a constant shape and is not distorted in the course of time. Is this anomaly real or does it correspond to an artificial situation?

The answer is obvious. It is absolutely unrealistic to speak of an harmonic oscillator with a strictly defined frequency. We never observe such an example. Every oscillator exhibits a large or small frequency band. It may be due to irregular fluctuations in the restoring force, or to some damping, but there is no spectral line of absolute purity. In spectroscopy, just a few spectral lines have been found pure enough to be used as frequency standards, and even these selected lines have always a finite and measurable width. Experimentally, we do not know any line of zero width, and a width of the order of 10^{-12} of the frequency seems to be the actual limit of accuracy.

Theoretically, all the oscillators we can think of are physical structures that are subject to fluctuations, and whose boundary conditions are not absolutely constant. We consider it unrealistic to speak of exact initial conditions. It is just as unrealistic to assume an exact frequency of oscillations. The frequency ν is defined with an error $\Delta\nu$. Let us wait a long time t and look for the phase φ of the oscillations

$$t = \left(n + \frac{\varphi}{2\pi}\right)\tau = \frac{1}{\nu}\left(n + \frac{\varphi}{2\pi}\right) \qquad n \text{ integer;} \quad \tau \text{ period}$$

or

$$\varphi = 2\pi(\nu t - n)$$

Assuming t large, and ν defined within an error $\Delta\nu$ the phase φ exhibits an error

$$\Delta\varphi = 2\pi t \Delta\nu \qquad\qquad\qquad (\text{VIII.10})$$

which may become as large as we wish. The situation is illustrated in Fig. 17.

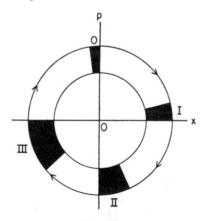

Fig. 17.

The Liouville theorem applies only if the restoring force is constant in time, and this is no more the case. There is no conservation of area for the Liouville surface element, which extends progressively until it entirely covers the whole region of possible motions. The uncertainty in the frequency restores here a situation similar to that obtained in other examples. It is well known that fluctuations in the restoring force (hence in the frequency) result from a variety of physical causes. For spectral lines, the role of the motion of atoms (Döppler effect) and of collisions with other atoms (finite wave trains) have been extensively studied, and do actually broaden the lines.

To summarize the problem, it is sufficient to note that an ideal oscillator (with $\Delta\nu = 0$) would be a perfect clock and allow for the measurement of time with infinite accuracy; and infinite accuracy is a physical impossibility.

7. THE PROBLEM OF DETERMINISM

The laws of classical mechanics represent a mathematical idealization and should not be assumed to correspond to the real laws of nature. In many problems (astronomy, for instance) they yield wonderful results that check with observation within experimental errors. In other fields they had to be amended (relativity, quantum mechanics). The classical viewpoint was to ignore the actual role and importance of experimental errors. Errors were assumed to be accidental; hence, it was always imagined that they could be made as small as one wished and finally ignored. This oversimplified picture led to the assumption of complete determinism in classical mechanics. We now have to realize that experimental errors are inevitable (see Section 2), a discovery that makes strict determinism impossible. Errors are an essential part of the world's picture and must be included in the theory.

Determinism must be replaced by statistical probabilities; a scientist may or may not believe in determinism. It is a matter of faith, and belongs to metaphysics. Physical discussions are unable to prove or to disprove it. This general viewpoint may be called the "matter of fact" position.

M. Born (1953, 1955, 1961) states the situation very clearly. He quotes Einstein (1953) as saying that, before quantum mechanics, it was assumed that "everything was to be reduced to objects situated in space-time, and to strict relations between these objects. . . . Nothing appeared to refer to our empirical knowledge about these objects. . . . This is what was meant by a physical description of a *real external world*." This position appears as untenable in modern physics. We have no way to prove the existence of such a real external world, and it is very dangerous to speak of something we cannot observe. If we restrain our thinking to observable facts, we can only speak of possible relations between a certain experiment and another one, but we should never discuss what happens while we are not making any observation; we must candidly admit that we do not know (no more than we know what happens on the other side of the moon).

Is such a viewpoint accepted by all physicists? The answer is far from clear. Pure mathematicians have great difficulty in agreeing with this inclusion of errors within the theory, and many theoretical physicists are still mathematicians at heart. The uncertainty relations of Bohr and Heisenberg are based upon the kind of thinking we tried to define. However, when one looks at the further expansion of quantum theories, he is amazed at the many fancy visualizations describing physics in terms of unobservable entities. The language of physicists is loaded with a jargon understandable only to specialists; special names have been coined for terms in a series of approximations, as if each isolated term had a meaning (exchange terms, pair creation, virtual creation and absorption of particles, etc.). Actually, only the final sum matters. Wise men know where and how to use these figures of language, and they are aware of their complete lack of reality. They realize that the jargon represents no more than an artificial way of describing complicated equations; but many physicists may be misled by such methods, which are really dangerous. In brief, quantum theory pays lip service to the sound principle of matter-of-fact descriptions, but soon forgets about it and uses a very careless language.

Besides mathematicians and quantum theoreticians, we find many scientists feeling very reluctant to face the situation described above, and to abandon old-fashioned ideas. They still believe in a real physical world following its own unperturbed evolution, whether we observe it or not. In order to reconcile this view with recent physical discoveries, they have to invent the existence of a number of "hidden variables" that we are unable to observe at present. In our opinion these hidden variables may do more harm than good. If we cannot observe them, let us admit that they have no reality and may exist only in the imagination of their authors. This is not meant as sarcasm. Imagination is absolutely needed in scientific research, and many important discoveries were, at the beginning, pure works of imagination; they became important only later when experimental proof was obtained and checked with results predicted by pure imagination. Finally, the new experimental discoveries became the scientific basis for the part that had been verified by experiment.

Quantum mechanics gave a wonderful description of the atomic and molecular structures, but did not succeed very well for field theory. As for newly discovered particles, they still remain very mysterious and it would be hard to predict the type of theory that may help in understanding them. For distances smaller than 10^{-13} cm, many new laws will have to be discovered. They are taking shape only bit by bit.

8. INFORMATION THEORY AND OUR PRECEDING EXAMPLES

All the examples discussed in Sections 4–6 are interesting to reexamine from the point of view of information theory. The position of the representative point in the x,p-plane is initially known within an area

$$A_0 = \Delta x_0 \Delta p_0 \tag{VIII.11}$$

If we do not change the accuracy of our measuring instruments, we must admit that the area does not practically remain constant (as was stated by Liouville) but actually increases progressively. This was shown in Figs. 10–17. After a long period of time, the uncertainty region practically covers the whole surface between inner and outer energy boundaries, as shown in Fig. 11. Hence, the area A increases until it reaches a final limit A_∞ given by the whole area of possible motions of energy E (within an error ΔE).

The information we have about the system is defined by the formula (VIII.7). The P_1 number is proportional to A and increases from A_0 to A_∞. The initial P_0 number depends upon experimental conditions. Let us assume a piece of apparatus where the position can vary from $-L$ to $+L$ while the momentum could take any value from $-P_m$ to $+P_m$. Such conditions would yield

$$P_0 = 4LP_m \tag{VIII.12}$$

This is similar to problems discussed in Chapter 20 of the book (Brillouin, 1956, 1962).

The information according to (VIII.7), for example, is

$$\Delta I = k(\log P_0 - \log P_1) = -k \log A + C' \tag{VIII.13}$$

a formula where $k \log P_0$ plays the role of an additional constant C', very similar to the additional constant in many entropy formulas.

In course of time, A increases from A_0 to A_∞ and the information decreases accordingly. The natural evolution of the system corresponds to a progressive

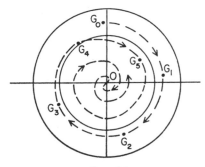

FIG. 18.

loss of information. Our general discussion leads directly to the law of loss of information (increase of entropy), which has provoked so many discussions since the time of Boltzmann. We had to renounce many classical assumptions; we showed the unphysical nature of determinism and maintained the "matter-of-fact" viewpoint. We thus obtained the fundamental law of entropy increase.

We can look at this problem from another angle and plot the motion of the center of gravity G of the area containing the representative point. This is shown in Fig. 18, which corresponds roughly to the problem of Fig. 17. The successive positions G_0, G_1, $G_2 \cdot \cdot \cdot$, describe a spiral which goes through the origin O when the shaded area covers exactly (for the first time) the whole area between the inner and outer energy circles. When the shaded areas overlap, the point G moves away from O and comes back to O again when the shaded area covers twice the circular ring, and so on.

If our moving particles are electrically charged, the oscillations of the center of gravity G will be visible by an emission of electromagnetic radiation and the wave train will exhibit an exponential damping with beats at t_1, t_2 and as shown in Fig. 19. When the time elapsed becomes very large, oscillations get

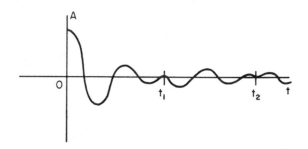

FIG. 19.

so small that they can no more be observed and the information has decreased to its lowest value.

$$\Delta I_\infty = C^t - k \log A_\infty \tag{VIII.14}$$

This discussion helps in visualizing the mechanism of natural loss of information.

The well-known arguments against Boltzmann stated by Loschmidt (reversibility) or Zermelo–Poincaré (recurrence) can be discarded as corresponding to nonphysical assumptions, impossible to realize in practice. Let us, for instance, consider the question of time reversibility. Particles are emitted (errors Δx and Δp) at time 0, as in Fig. 10. At a certain time t_1 all velocities are suddenly reversed (how to do it is another question!); the particles travel backward and regroup together at time $2t_1$, rebuilding the original signal. If this could actually be done, irreversibility would be disproved. However, we have emphasized the *impossibility of ignoring experimental errors*, and there are many points where they come in:

(A) The reversal time t_1 is defined within an error Δt_1; hence, the signal is rebuilt at $2t_1$ with an error $2\Delta t_1$.

(B) The reversal is not rigorously obtained. Original particles were moving in the x direction, for instance, and reflected particles will have small transverse velocities $v_y v_z$. They will come back to the origin within a distance $2t_1 v_y$ and $2t_1 v_z$, these errors increasing with t_1.

(C) The field of forces through which particles are moving cannot be kept rigorously independent of time. It will exhibit fluctuations (as in the problem of Section 6, Fig. 16). These fluctuations make the Liouville theorem invalid and also destroy the reversibility.

Altogether, the idea of reversibility in mechanical motions is just a dream and cannot be checked exactly, on account of experimental errors, which become larger and larger when the reversal time t_1 increases progressively. Even in classical mechanics, time's arrow cannot be reversed.

The only known example of reversal was discovered by E. L. Hahn (1950) with spin echoes and exhibits the characteristics specified here. Echoes get smaller and less sharp when reversal time is increased. Exact reversal and exact reversibility are out of question.

9. OBSERVATION AND INTERPRETATION

The point of view presented in this paper can be compared with the discussion at a meeting held in Bristol (Körner, 1957) where philosophers and physicists compared opinions on "Observation and Interpretation." Theory belongs to the interpretation of experiments, and the whole problem is: how much is added to experimental facts (and hence liable to misunderstandings), and how can we distinguish these creations of our imagination from actual observations? Can we even eliminate the imaginative elements and maintain strictly the "matter-of-fact" point of view advocated in the preceding sections?

We recognized in Section 7, that theory is a work of imagination, first built on a few arbitrary guesses, later compared with observation. If experimental facts check with theoretical predictions, the usefulness of the theory is proven but this does not mean that all the original guesses (or postulates) are right. Many historical discussions exemplify the contrary: the elastic theory of light assumed an "ether" with very strange properties. It was replaced by the electromagnetic theory of Maxwell (still with another strange ether) and finally the ether was discarded as nonsense by Einstein. Now we have the quantized field theory, which certainly contains many nonobservable features, and can hardly be considered as a finished piece of theory. In these successive transformations, the imaginative elements were completely different, but the amount of experimental territory covered was progressively extended.

Theory is like a map of reality, it is not a correct and complete description of the world. We start with a plane map, then we modify it to include the rotundity of the earth, and step by step we improve our representation, but this is a job never ended and never finished.

At each stage of a theory some scientists pretend to prove that the theory is perfect, and that it is not possible to modify it in any way. The only thing they can prove is that the theory is consistent, logically built, and checks with experimental evidence over a certain limited ground. Very soon, however, new empirical facts will be discovered which require a complete reshaping of theories. Quantum theories were supposedly proven to be the final word,[1] yet now they are unable to explain all the strange new particles recently discovered, not to speak of the problems of nuclear structures.

At the Bristol symposium, L. Rosenfeld discussed (Körner, 1957, p. 41) the foundations of quantum theory and presented the Copenhagen point of view, which is very close to the general positions taken by M. Born and the present writer. In the opposite camp, D. Bohm attempted to justify theories playing with unobservable variables, and discussions between both groups were very lively. Everybody agreed that many strange things appear at distances smaller than 10^{-13} cm, but their theoretical explanation is still to be discovered. The Rosenfeld report should be especially commended as particularly clear and aiming at economy in undefined postulates. Two reports of the Bristol meeting (Feyeraband and Sussmann) deal with the theory of measurement and seem to be more interested in logical formalism than in actual experiments. It is curious to note that experimental errors are practically ignored in these reports; the first one is essentially based on von Neumann's formal analysis, whereas the second one emphasizes the role of Schrödinger waves and discusses the "quantum jumps" provoked by coupling the observed system to the measuring device. Many of the remarks made in the discussion of these reports seem rather artificial because they omit experimental errors, background noise in the observations, noise in the amplifiers, etc. Experts in information theory know the importance of these factors, which were almost completely overlooked in the Bristol symposium.

Many other points of importance should be raised about the Bristol meeting, in connection with "scientific prediction" and quantum theory description, but it seems such a discussion would take us too far away from our main objective. Let us strongly suggest that the reader study these most interesting reports.

10. CONCLUSIONS

A short conclusion may be useful, and give a summary of this Chapter.

(A) *Experimental errors are inevitable*, and it is unscientific to think of infinite accuracy in any measurement. This limitation is already present in classical theories (M. Born), and is formulated in precise ways by quantum conditions and information theory (Section 2).

(B) Some simple *examples* are discussed in Sections 3–5, and show the type of uncertainties encountered even in classical models.

[1] Many discussions of a famous theorem of von Neumann may be found in Körner (1957, pp. 33, 47, 140) and represent a striking example of our remarks.

(C) The inevitable errors must be included in the theory, since they are an essential part of our knowledge of the world around us. This makes *strict determinism impossible* in scientific prediction. Laplace's demon cannot make accurate measurements and is unable to predict the future exactly (Sections 3 and 7). This is what we called the "matter-of-fact" point of view.

(D) The natural evolution of a system corresponds to a *loss of information*, hence an increase of entropy (Section 8). Similar problems were discussed at the Bristol symposium.

REFERENCES

Borel, E. (1925). "Mécanique statistique classique" (Lectures written by Fr. Perrin), p. 22. Gauthier-Villars, Paris.

Born, M. (1953). Physical reality. *Phil. Quart.* 3, 139.

Born, M. (1955). Continuity, determinism and reality. *Kgl. Danske Videnskab Selskab. Mat.-fys. Medd.* 30, No. 2.

Born, M. (1961). Bemerkungen zur Statistischen Deutung der Quantenmechanik. In the Jubilee Volume "Werner Heisenberg und die Physik unserer Zeit," p. 103. Vieweg, Braunschweig.

Brillouin, L. (1956). "Science and Information Theory," 1st ed., especially Chapters 16 and 20. Academic Press, New York.

Brillouin, L. (1957). Mathematics, physics and information (an Editorial). *Inform. & Control* 1, 1–5.

Brillouin, L. (1958). Information theory and divergent sums in physics. *Ann. Phys.* 5, 243.

Brillouin, L. (1959). Inevitable experimental errors, determinism, and information theory. *Inform. & Control* 2, 45.

Brillouin, L. (1962). "Science and Information Theory," 2nd ed., Chapter 22. Academic Press, New York.

Einstein, A. (1953). "Scientific Papers presented to M. Born," p. 33. Oliver & Boyd, London.

Hahn, E. L. (1950). *Phys. Rev.* 80, 580.

Korner, S., ed. (1957). "Observations and Interpretation. A Symposium of Philosophers and Physicists," Proc. of the Ninth Symposium of the Colston Research Society held in the University of Bristol. Academic Press, New York.

Schrödinger, E. (1954). "Nature and the Greeks," Chapter VII. Cambridge Univ. Press, London and New York.

Chapter IX

POINCARÉ AND THE SHORTCOMINGS OF THE HAMILTON–JACOBI METHOD FOR CLASSICAL OR QUANTIZED MECHANICS[1]

1. POINCARÉ'S "SCIENCE AND HYPOTHESIS"

Famous old authors are always worth rereading. Let us open Poincaré's (1902) book "Science and Hypothesis" to Chapter VIII, where the author discusses the definition of "energy"; we find on page 158 (French edition, or page 121, English edition) a very curious problem stated in the following way:

> In the determinist hypothesis, the state of the universe is determined by an extremely great number n of parameters which I shall call $x_1, x_2, \ldots, x_n$. As soon as the values of these n parameters at any instant are known, their derivatives with respect to time are likewise known, and consequently the values of these same parameters at a preceding or subsequent instant can be calculated. In other words, these n parameters satisfy n differential equations of the first order.
>
> These equations admit of $n - 1$ integrals, and consequently there are $n - 1$ functions of $x_1, x_2, \ldots, x_n$, which remain constant. *If then we say there is something which remains constant, we only*

[1] Revised from a paper by the author first published in *Arch. Rational Mech. Anal.* **5**, No. 1, 76–94. (1960).

utter a tautology. We should even be puzzled to say which among all our integrals should retain the name of energy.

Poincaré presents there, in a paradoxical way, a very profound problem. In a private letter (December 1958), Schrödinger writes:

December 29th, 1958

Dear Brillouin,

. . . Many thanks for your new book on information theory, which came a little while ago (Brillouin, 1958). . . .

I took at once from my shelf my very old copy (still among my father's books) of Poincaré's "Science et Hypothèse" and read the 8th Chapter "Energie et Thermodynamique." This is extraordinary! Yet, I do not think the author was as naive as he makes one feel. In the first place *énergétique* must have meant at that time in France something very different from Ostwald's hobby *Energetik* (against which Boltzmann fought battles). But then, one is amazed to find Poincaré taking "forces at a distance" quite seriously, in particular also Weber's forces that depend on the velocity. Poincaré surely knew about Maxwell's theory, nay, some people (with, maybe, slight exaggeration) claim for Poincaré if not *priorité*, at any rate important contribution prior to Einstein on the question of restricted relativity. . . . I thought for a moment that this 8th Chapter might have been written down *much* earlier and was allowed to be included by an elderly man, who just did not care. But that cannot be, for in 1902 Henri Poincaré was at the youthful age of 48 (alas, he died ten years later, in 1912). A man in full vigor will not have anything printed that is far from his present views. My only explanation, then, is that Poincaré is sort of pulling his reader's leg (by ostensibly adopting antiquated ideas) in order to explain in the simplest way some very new and relevant points of view, in particular this: if some function of the co-ordinates and momenta is a constant of the motion (say $\mathscr{H}$), then any function $f(\mathscr{H})$ also is, and we must show a reason to call $\mathscr{H}$ the energy rather than any particular $f(\mathscr{H})$. And similarly: in the ordinary case of classical mechanics, there is not just *one* constant of the motion, but $n - 1$. Which of them is the energy? Or rather, what function of those $n - 1$? I believe these were, certainly at that time, points very worth making, and perhaps worth thinking about even now. We have become used to expressing the energy principle by saying that the sum of adduced heat and impressed labor for driving a system from state 1 to state 2 is independent of the way in which we perform the transition. That is easily said and easily taken in. But few of our younger people realize the difficulty of measuring the "imparted heat" at the successive steps. This is quite an involved epistemological problem, implying the measurement of the specific heats of various bodies at various temperatures (Mach has dealt with these things in his "Theory of Heat"), and it is imperative to ask oneself whether, *en fin du conte*, one has stated a tautology or something better. However that may be, in turning the leaves following this 8th Chapter, one becomes fully convinced that H. Poincaré was very much more up to date in his thinking about physics than would appear from that Chapter 8.

Heartiest greetings, yours as ever,

(Signed) E. Schrödinger

We intend to discuss the preceding problem, and we shall compare it with a very important theorem discovered by Poincaré (1892–1899) himself in his work on celestial mechanics, which contains a very pertinent answer to the problem. This will lead us into a discussion of the limits of accuracy in classical mechanics, and of the foundations of statistical mechanics. The problem was originally intended by Poincaré to apply to a general physical system, but his statement certainly cannot be used for a quantized structure since it does not include any possibility of quantum jumps. Hence we shall restrict the discussion to a *classical mechanical system*. We thus examine the following problem:

We consider a *conservative mechanical system*, with neither dissipation (no friction, no passive resistance) nor regeneration [no external energy source, no negative (active) resistance]. For such a model we easily define potential and kinetic energy, hence total energy too. This is the way all problems of classical mechanics are usually stated. Poincaré himself, when discussing a celestial problem, has no hesitation about how to write down the total energy of the system.

There are N coordinates x_1, x_2, ..., x_N and N corresponding momenta p_1, ..., p_N. This represents the n parameters of Poincaré:

$$n = 2N \qquad \text{(IX.1)}$$

The initial state of the system at $t = 0$ is defined when we give the initial values $x_1(0)$, ..., $x_N(0)$, $p_1(0)$, ..., $p_N(0)$ of the $2N$ parameters. The mathematician considers these initial values as "given," but the physicist asks "Given by whom?" We must enquire how these initial values are measured and investigate the accuracy. This involves a complete change of point of view, and here we quote a remark of Hadamard: "The question is not whether you make a very small change in the initial conditions, the real problem is whether this small initial change may not result in a very large change in the final results." In other words, the problem concerns the stability of the trajectories.

From $t = 0$ on, the system moves on according to the laws of mechanics, and we may compute the coordinates $x_i(t)$ and momenta $p_i(t)$ at time t. These $2N$ quantities are defined in terms of one variable t and $(2N - 1)$ constants, to be computed from the initial conditions. These $2N - 1$ constants are the "first integrals" considered by Poincaré in his paradoxical statement in "Science and Hypothesis."

2. POINCARÉ'S GREAT THEOREM ON CELESTIAL MECHANICS

Let us now open a previous book of Poincaré himself (1892–1899), the first volume of his "Méthodes nouvelles de la mécanique céleste," and read Chapter V, entitled, "Nonexistence of Uniform Integrals." The whole chapter is devoted to the discussion of one fundamental theorem:

The canonical equations of celestial mechanics do not admit (except for some exceptional cases to be discussed separately) any analytical and uniform integral besides the energy integral.

This great Poincaré theorem contains the answer to the previous problem. It definitely proves that the $(n - 1)$ integrals previously introduced by Poincaré have very different properties. The total energy is the only expression which is represented by a "well-behaved" mathematical function, and all other so-called integrals are not analytical; they may have a very strange behavior, with discontinuities, and cannot be compared with the energy. The integrals representing momentum, or moment of momentum (if they exist), are comprised in the other "exceptional cases" discussed by Poincaré.

For instance, Poincaré applies his theorem to the three-body problem (Vol. I, p. 253). Assuming the center of mass to remain at rest, there are four actual first integrals, corresponding to moment of momentum and energy; Poincaré's theorem proves that no other well-behaved first integral can be found, and it thus puts an end to a century of unsuccessful attempts.

Why did Poincaré choose not to mention this great theorem in his later book? The reason must be that in "Science and Hypothesis" he had in mind a much more general problem, and was thinking of the behavior of any arbitrary physical system; but we already said that his statement certainly does not hold for quantum theory and that the problem must be restricted to classical mechanics only.

Our aim is to compare this theorem with the original statement of Poincaré, and in doing so, we have to present a short summary of the standard methods of analytical dynamics. We choose to follow an excellent textbook written by Max Born (1925) on atom mechanics, where the classical methods are very precisely discussed for the problems of the "old" quantized mechanics, for which they represented the skeleton of the theory.

This text is also chosen because of a curious coincidence: after discussing very precisely the Hamilton–Jacobi method, and using it for computation on perturbed systems, M. Born considers the great Poincaré theorem, which apparently contradicts the "general" perturbation methods of M. Born and restricts their validity to the exceptional cases where the theorem does not apply. Born just quotes two theorems of Bruns and Poincaré (p. 292). Both theorems refer to the convergence of expansions obtained by the perturbation theory. The theorem of Bruns (1884) states that points of absolute convergence or of divergence are equally dense. The perturbation procedure introduces nonanalytic functions on one side and assumes the property of analyticity at another point: it thus contains internal contradictions. Poincaré's theorem also refers to perturbation methods in celestial mechanics and goes further than Bruns'. Born mentions these grave difficulties and does not elaborate further (he must have been too busy at the time with the "matrix mechanics" he was inventing with Heisenberg). He nevertheless adds some interesting comments: "It thus was never possible to prove the stability of the solar system. . . . The perturbation methods used in celestial mechanics are not convergent, but only semiconvergent (Poincaré, Vol. II, Chapter VIII). *We thus see that it is impossible, for purely theoretical reasons, to prove the absolute stability of atomic systems.*" Let us add that these semiclassical methods completely failed in the case of the helium atom.

For atomic structures, the solution was found with the invention of wave mechanics, which considers the old-fashioned quantized mechanics only as a first approximation of limited validity. The well-known B.W.K. method gives the connection between both methods, but fails on Poincaré's discontinuities (See Chapter X).

We shall first remind the reader of the fundamental methods of classical mechanics, in order to be in a position to discuss the importance of Poincaré's theorem and to examine the limitations it introduces upon the validity of classical methods.

3. The Methods of Analytical Dynamics for Separated Variables

As stated in the preceding section, we refer the reader to Born's textbook for all details, and we shall be satisfied with a short summary of the general situation; quotations will be distinguished by a B (for Born).

If we have *just one variable* ($N = 1$), there is only one

$$2N - 1 = 1 \tag{IX.2}$$

first integral, which will directly define the energy. *Assuming stability*, the motion is periodic, and we introduce an angular variable w, of which both x and p are periodic functions (period 2π)

$$w = vt + w_0 \tag{IX.3}$$

During one period, w increases by one unit.

The corresponding momentum is the action variable

$$J = \oint p\,dx \qquad (IX.4)$$

taken for a full period. The energy depends only upon J

$$E = E(J) \qquad (IX.5)$$

and the equation of motion yields

$$\frac{dw}{dt} = v = \frac{\partial E}{\partial J} \qquad (IX.6)$$

where v is the classical frequency. The action J was chosen for quantization, and the old quantized mechanics used the assumption

$$J = nh, \qquad n \text{ an integer} \qquad (IX.7)$$

with a quantum frequency

$$v_q = \frac{\Delta E}{h} = \frac{\Delta E}{\Delta J} \qquad \Delta J = h \qquad (IX.8)$$

The similarity of Eqs. (IX.6) and (IX.8) was the basis of Bohr's *correspondence* principle. On the other hand, it was proven that any slow change of a parameter in the energy formula would leave J (and hence n) unchanged. This is the *principle of adiabatic invariance* (B., Chapter II, paragraphs 1–12) which applies *as long as the frequency v does not become zero*.

These formulas can be easily generalized for a stable system with *separable variables*.[1] This is the case when the independent variables $x_1, \ldots, x_K$ can be chosen in such a way that each pair x_K, p_K obeys a separate equation of motion and is periodic with a frequency v_k (the period being $\tau_k = 1/v_k$). We have Eqs. (IX.3), (IX.4), (IX.6), and (IX.7) as before (each one being given a subscript k), and the total energy, instead of equation (IX.5), is given by an expression

$$E = E(J_1, J_2, \ldots, J_N) \qquad (IX.9)$$

containing only the action variables J. Such a stable system is called *multi-*

---

[1] Born, M.: Chapter II, paragraphs 14–17. Beware of the fact that Born uses different notations:

	Born	Here
Frequency	v_k	v_k
Period	ω_k	τ_k
Integer	τ_k	m_k

periodic. If we consider a quantity represented by a function of the variables x_k, p_k, it can be rewritten as a function of the angular variables w_k

$$F(w_1, w_2, \ldots, w_N)$$

and it exhibits period 1 in each of the w_K variables. These variables themselves are linear functions of time (Eq. (IX.3)) and the function F can be expanded in a multiple Fourier series

$$F = \sum_m C_m e^{2\pi i (m \cdot w)} = \sum_m C_m e^{2\pi i t (m \cdot v) + 2\pi i (m \cdot w_0)} \tag{IX.10}$$

where m represents a set of integers $m_1, m_2, \ldots, m_N$, and $(m \cdot w)$ or $(m \cdot v)$ are scalar products

$$(m \cdot w) = \sum_k m_k \cdot w_k \qquad (m \cdot v) = \sum_k (m_k \cdot v_k)$$

The system is *nondegenerate* if *no relation*

$$(m \cdot v) = 0 \qquad m \text{ integers} \tag{IX.11}$$

can be found; otherwise it is called *degenerate.* In such a case, the number of independent angular variables is reduced. If we have n relations Eq. (IX.11), the number of independent frequencies is $N - n$. The system is completely degenerate when there remains only one angular variable and one frequency v. This is the case, for instance, for Kepler ellipses or for Lissajoux figures.

The condition (IX.11) for nondegeneracy is very restrictive. It means that all frequencies are incommensurable, so that there exists no zero combination frequency among them. On the other hand, some *quasi-periods* τ_q (Poincaré) can be found that satisfy relations

$$\tau_q = m_1 \tau_1 + \epsilon_1 = m_2 \tau_2 + \epsilon_2 \cdots = m_N \tau_N + \epsilon_N \tag{IX.12}$$

with errors $\epsilon_1, \epsilon_2, \ldots, \epsilon_N$ as small as desired. If all the ϵ were zero for a certain choice of the m_K's, the τ would really be a common period and the system would completely degenerate, since Eq. (IX.12) could be written

$$\frac{v_1}{m_1} = \frac{v_2}{m_2} \cdots \frac{v_N}{m_N} = v = \frac{1}{\tau_q} \tag{IX.13}$$

which represents $N - 1$ rational relations between the original periods v_K.

In the old quantized mechanics, the J action variables corresponding to the w's were quantized, according to Eq. (IX.7). These J's were *adiabatic invariants* for any slow change of a parameter in the equations, *so long as the nondegeneracy was maintained and no condition* (IX.11) would occur between the frequencies slowly modified by the change of the parameter. This condition of no degeneracy is so restrictive as to make the *invariance very seldom applicable.*

The reason that degeneracy may raise difficulties must be investigated carefully. This will be done in the following sections. Right now, we may explain that trouble will arise wherever variables do not remain strictly separated. The variation of a parameter of the problem may perturb the separation, hence raising troubles at points of degeneracy.

It may, however, happen that the change of the parameter does not establish any coupling between the separate variables, instead maintaining complete independence of their equations. If such were the case, the occasional degeneracy would no longer be an obstacle.

Coming back to our equations with separated variables, we note that the system has $2N - 1$ integrals, namely the N action variables J_K (which define the energy) and the $N - 1$ phase differences ($w_{k0} - w_{10}$).

These are the constants considered in Section 1. Their respective importance and their general behavior will be discussed later.

4. Nonseparable Variables. Hamilton–Jacobi Procedure

When variables cannot be separated, the problem becomes much more involved. One may try a formal solution, based on Hamilton–Jacobi equations, or one wishes to be more practical and to use a method of approximation.

We restrict our discussion to the case of *stable problems*, when no particle may go to infinity.

The Hamilton–Jacobi equations yield a possibility of finding angular variables w_k and the corresponding action variables J_K which formally satisfy equations very similar to those of the preceding section. These variables are often called Delaunay variables. A typical feature results from the fact that this procedure now involves a "contact transformation" instead of a "point transformation." The Poincaré theorem of Section 2 will play a distinctive role in emphasizing the difficulties of this general theory. The classical application of the Hamilton–Jacobi method is given by Born (B., Paragraphs 5–8, 15), and the discussion proves that difficulties arise whenever a degeneracy condition (IX.11) obtains. This means that the *definition of the w, J variables may be materially* altered at points of degeneracy.

Such a restriction was easily eliminated in a problem with separated variables, because there was no coupling possible between different variables. Here one must admit that this sort of coupling does exist in general, and that occasional degeneracy must cause trouble.

At any rate, the Hamilton–Jacobi procedure has never been a way to solve a practical problem. It is very useful for general theorems and elegant discussions, but not for actual solution.

5. Successive Approximations

The only available method for the solution of a special problem is the *method of successive approximations* (B., Sections 18, 34–35 and 40–44). In introducing the method, it is necessary to start with the case of degeneracy (B., Section 18). We assume an unperturbed energy function given by the Hamiltonian H_0 and a small perturbation λH_1 (λ small),

$$H = H_0 + \lambda H_1 \tag{IX.14}$$

The problem is supposed to have been already solved for the unperturbed Hamiltonian H_0, and it may yield a partly degenerate solution. The small perturbation is usually enough to remove the degeneracy. For instance, the initial problem, being n times degenerate, depends only upon $N - n$ angular variables [see Section 3, Eq. (IX.11)] and obtains that many actual frequencies, while n frequencies are zero. When the degeneracy is lifted, the $N - n$ original frequencies are modified by an amount proportional to λ, while the n additional frequencies take small nonzero values of the order of λ. Each perturbation function H_1 will react differently on the n degenerate degrees of freedom, and result in a different choice for these additional w and J variables. Hence we see directly how a *point of degeneracy* will be a point for *possible sudden changes in the definition of angular and action variables.*

Let us consider a nondegenerate system characterized by a perturbation term λH_1, and the corresponding w, J variables. Then, let us decrease λ to zero and produce degeneracy; finally we introduce another perturbation $\lambda' H_1'$, which will result in a different choice of angular variables w' and action variables J'. The original J's were adiabatic invariants for a slow change of λ; for $\lambda = 0$ we have a sudden change in the J values, and the new J's are adiabatic invariants for a slow variation of λ'.

A well-known example in atomic models is represented by an atom first perturbed by a magnetic field (Zeeman effect, B., Paragraph 34) and then by an electric field (Stark, B., Paragraph 35).

To be more specific, let us assume a system with 2 degrees of freedom which both yield the same frequency ν_0 in the unperturbed problem. This may be a Kepler ellipse where r and θ have the same frequency ν_0. The same ellipse may also be represented in x, y coordinates, and they have again the same frequency ν_0. The first perturbation λH_1 may separate r and θ, giving them frequencies ν_r and ν_θ, both slightly different from ν_0; the difference $\nu_r - \nu_\theta$ represents the frequency which is zero in the degenerate case and becomes a small quantity of the order of λ in the perturbed problem. The second perturbation $\lambda' H'$ may be a field in the x direction, acting differently on x or y and producing frequencies ν_x and ν_y. In both cases, action variables are easily found. The transformation $\lambda H_1 \rightarrow \lambda' H_1'$ exhibits continuity of the frequencies $\quad\nu_r, \nu_\theta \to \nu_0 \to \nu_x, \nu_y$ $\quad$ (IX.15)

discontinuity in the action variables $\quad J_r, J_\theta \neq J_x, J_y$

The formulas (IX.6) for the frequencies are always valid despite the discontinuous change in the J variables:

$$\nu_r = \frac{\partial H_0}{\partial J_r} + \lambda\frac{\partial H_1}{\partial J_r} = \nu_0 + \lambda\frac{\partial H_1}{\partial J_r}$$

$$\nu_\theta = \nu_0 + \lambda\frac{\partial H_1}{\partial J_\theta} \tag{IX.16}$$

$$\nu_x = \nu_0 + \lambda'\frac{\partial H_1'}{\partial J_x}$$

$$\nu_y = \nu_0 + \lambda'\frac{\partial H_1'}{\partial J_y}$$

We have oversimplified the problem in order to show more clearly the fundamental mechanism involved. Let us generalize and assume a degeneracy of the type

$$m_1\nu_1 - m_2\nu_2 = 0 \quad m_1 > 0 \quad m_2 > 0 \quad \text{integers} \tag{IX.17}$$

hence with the periods

$$\tau_1 = m_1\tau, \quad \tau_2 = m_2\tau$$

$$\tau = \frac{1}{\nu} = \frac{1}{m_1\nu_1} = \frac{1}{m_2\nu_2}$$

The action integral J at degeneracy is related to $J_1 J_2$ before degeneracy by the formula

$$J = \oint_\tau (p_1 dx_1 + p_2 dx_2) = \frac{1}{m_1}J_1 + \frac{1}{m_2}J_2 \tag{IX.18}$$

This relation shows the J discontinuity.

6. APPROXIMATIONS FOR NONDEGENERATE SYSTEMS

The preceding problem actually represents the general case. When we start from a nondegenerate system and modify, even very slightly, any parameter, we immediately pass through a very large number of degenerate situations. *Nondegeneracy* requires a set of incommensurable frequencies. We already noticed, in Section 3, that adiabatic invariance of the action variables could be proven only so long as nondegeneracy was obtained, or separation of variables maintained, preventing any coupling between different groups of variables. In the general case, we cannot assume complete separation, and the slightest perturbation destroys the nondegeneracy; hence the definition of angle and action variables becomes hopeless. It may have to be changed at each point of degeneracy, and these points lie infinitely close to each other. This essential difficulty is easily recognized in the general discussion sketched by Born (B., Paragraph 41). Assuming a Hamiltonian of the type

$$H = H_0 + \lambda H_1 + \lambda^2 H_2 \ldots \qquad \lambda \text{ small} \qquad \text{(IX.19)}$$

where H_0 is the unperturbed Hamiltonian and $H_1, H_2, \ldots$ are perturbation functions, the resolution requires the formation of a transformation function

$$S = S_0 + \lambda S_1 + \lambda^2 S_2 \ldots \qquad \text{(IX.20)}$$

and the successive terms S_1, S_2 are found to be of the general type (B., p.290)

$$S_n = \sum_m{}' \frac{1}{2\pi i} \frac{A_m}{(m \cdot v_0)} e^{2\pi i (m \cdot w)} \qquad \text{(with no constant term)} \qquad \text{(IX.21)}$$

a formula where $(m \cdot v_0)$ and $(m \cdot w)$ represent scalar products defined for Eq. (IX.10), while the A_m coefficient is computed from $H_1, H_2 \ldots$ perturbation functions. If the system is originally nondegenerate, then no denominator $(m \cdot v_0)$ can be identically zero, and Born assumes that the expansion is convergent. The case is not that simple since a great many denominators will be as nearly zero as desired (or rather, as *not* desired).

These extremely small denominators may make the sum divergent; and we must add that the smallest perturbation would make some of these $(m \cdot v)$ actually zero and S_n infinite. The perturbed action variables J are defined in terms of the S function and thus are open to any kind of irregular behavior and discontinuities. The frequencies are again continuous. This situation will help us understand the exact meaning of the great Poincaré theorem.

In the preceding discussion, it was assumed that degeneracy or nondegeneracy was directly controlled by the nature of the Hamiltonian. Let us remember that *initial conditions* of the motion also play a decisive role. For instance, the frequency of a physical pendulum is a function of amplitude; if we have a pendulum oscillating along x and y, with different nonlinear restoring forces in both directions, we easily see that the frequencies v_x and v_y can be made commensurable or incommensurable by very small changes of the initial conditions. Hence initial conditions also control degeneracy. This point will be of importance for later discussion.

7. Poincaré's Great Theorem Again

We must now come back to Poincaré's great theorem, which we quoted in Section 2 without examining carefully its meaning and importance. The importance of this theorem is well recognized by astronomers, but mathematicians and physicists often overlook it; its implications reach very far and shatter many current ideas in classical mechanics. Let us first explain the exact statement of Poincaré. He considers a mechanical system obeying the canonical equations

$$\frac{dx_i}{dt} = \frac{\partial F}{\partial y_i} \qquad \frac{dy_i}{dt} = -\frac{\partial F}{\partial x_i} \qquad \text{(IX.22)}$$

where $x_1, \ldots, x_i, \ldots, x_N$ are the variables and $y_1, \ldots, y_i, \ldots, y_N$ are the corresponding moments, while $F(x_i, y_i)$ is the total energy of the system. The special problem considered by Poincaré is the three-body problem of celestial mechanics, and the energy F is supposed to be expanded in power series of a certain parameter μ

$$F = F_0 + \mu F_1 + \mu^2 F_2 + \cdots \qquad \text{(IX.23)}$$

This represents a typical case of perturbation, and the μ expansion of equation (IX.23) corresponds to the λ expansion of our previous equation (IX.19), since H or F both represent the total energy. What is different in Poincaré's case is the choice of the x_i, y_i variables.

In the unperturbed problem, it is assumed that F_0 depends upon the N variables x_i but not upon the y_i's. The perturbation functions $F_1, F_2 \ldots$ depend upon both x_i and y_i variables. Furthermore, the whole problem is multiperiodic (hence stable), and here is how it happens:

The mechanical equations (IX.22) give, in the unperturbed problem,

$$x_i = x_{i0} \text{ constant} \qquad y_i = -\frac{\partial F}{\partial x_i} t + y_{i0} \qquad \text{(IX.24)}$$

and the original coordinates of the system (Poincaré, *loc. cit.*, pp. 22–32) are multiperiodic functions of the y_i's. Hence the y_i (momentum variables) play the role of our previous w_i (angular variables) while the x_i variables replace the previous action variables. Finally, the situation is exactly similar to the previous problem, with just an interchange of variables and momenta, and such an interchange is known to be of no consequence whatsoever.

Accepting y_i as representing an angular variable w_i, we see that

$$-\frac{\partial F}{\partial x_i} = v_i \qquad \text{(IX.25)}$$

is the corresponding frequency. (There is, however, a different use of the 2π factors in the treatments of Born and Poincaré, but this again is immaterial.)

The system is multiperiodic with respect to the y_i variables, and this is also true for the F_1, F_2 perturbation terms.

With these assumptions, Poincaré explains the precise meaning of his theorem:

Let φ be an analytic and uniform function of x, y, μ which must also be periodic with respect to the y variables. Let this function φ be supposed to be analytic and uniform for all values of the y's, for small values of μ, and for

x's contained in a certain domain D. Under such conditions, the function φ can be expanded

$$\varphi = \varphi_0 + \mu\varphi_1 + \mu^2\varphi_2 + \cdots \tag{IX.26}$$

with $\varphi_0, \varphi_1, \varphi_2, \ldots$ uniform in x, y and periodic in the y's. Poincaré then states: *Except for some special cases to be discussed later, such a function cannot be an integral of the system of equations* (IX.22). *Only the total energy F has such properties.*

This theorem invalidates the system of approximations developed by Born, who tried to find expansions of type (IX.26) for his action variables J in a perturbed problem by using a transformation function S also expanded in a similar fashion. The S and J's cannot be well-behaved analytic functions. This is the very remarkable consequence of Poincaré's theorem.

We do not intend to repeat here the details of the proof given by Poincaré, but we shall stress a few points of importance, since they explain clearly that all the trouble comes from points of *degeneracy*, which also give difficulties in Born's discussion. This *old theorem* of Poincaré proves that these difficulties are much more serious than was imagined and that they build up an almost impassable roadblock.

8. The Role of Degeneracy Conditions in Poincaré's Theorem

The clue, in Poincaré's discussion, is to consider, for each stage of approximation, the behavior of the function φ at the points of degeneracy. These points are defined by conditions

$$\sum m_i \frac{\partial F_0}{\partial x_i} = \sum m_i \nu_i = 0, \qquad m_i \text{ integers} \tag{IX.27}$$

according to (IX.25). And Poincaré notes that, in any domain of the x_i's, even the smallest domain you can imagine, there is always an infinity of such points of commensurability (or degeneracy; see, for instance, Poincaré, p. 239, bottom of the page).

The perturbation function F_1 is expanded in multiple Fourier series (Poincaré, pp. 236–238),

$$F_1 = \sum B_m e^{2\pi i (m \cdot y)} \tag{IX.28}$$

a formula similar to our equation (IX.10). The general case refers to a perturbation F_1 that may contain all the B_m terms. In such a case, the proof shows that the function φ cannot exist. When some of the B coefficients are zero, the discussion runs differently (Poincaré, pp. 240–245) since there is a possibility of secular perturbation. For certain classes of problems, it is still possible to prove the great Poincaré theorem, but for another group of problems, there appears a possibility of finding a certain limited number of well-behaved first integrals, in addition to the energy integral. These are the exceptional cases announced by Poincaré in the statement of his theorem. These exceptional cases practically correspond to problems where a limited number of sets of variables can be separated away.

A typical example corresponds to a problem with conservation of the total momentum or moment of momentum.

There are many other interesting remarks to be found in Poincaré's admirable book, and they apply not only to celestial mechanics but to general mechanical problems. In his third volume (Chapters 28–31), Poincaré defines *periodic solutions of the second kind*, which correspond to another example of degeneracy: some trajectories exhibit a period τ, but other trajectories, very close to the first ones, may not be periodic at all or may have a much longer period $n\tau$, a multiple of the original τ. An example of these conditions was found in the problem of degeneracy discussed in equations (IX.17) and (IX.18).

We can say, in concluding these two sections, that the very fundamental properties discovered by Poincaré in his great theorem are provoked by degeneracy conditions when the Hamiltonian gives rise to coupling between the different sets of variables.

9. Degeneracy Conditions and the Possibility of Finding a Hamilton–Jacobi Transformation Function

We shall now generalize the preceding remarks and show that the Hamilton–Jacobi transformation function S itself may, in general, be very difficult or even impossible to obtain. We shall prove that the Hamilton–Jacobi method works wonderfully for separated variables but usually becomes impracticable when the variables are not separable.

We start from the following formulas, which can be taken as a definition of the transformation function S (S was called F in Brillouin's (1938, 1964) book on tensors) of Eq. (IX.20)

$$\frac{\partial S}{\partial q_k} = p_k \qquad \text{hence} \qquad dS = \sum \frac{\partial S}{\partial q_k} dq_k = \sum p_k dq_k \qquad \text{(IX.29)}$$

We thus can write

$$S = \int_{q_{k0}}^{q_k} p_k dq_k = \int_{q_{k0}}^{q_k} p_k \dot{q}_k dt = \int_{q_{k0}}^{q_k} 2E_{\text{kin}} dt \qquad \text{(IX.30)}$$

The kinetic energy E_{kin} was called T in the book. The integral is taken along a natural trajectory running from an initial point q_{k0} at $t = 0$ to a final point q_k at t. This integral is completely defined when we specify the total energy E of the system under consideration; once we know E, and we give the position $q_k(t)$ at time t, then the potential energy $V(q_k)$ is known, and the difference $E - V$ gives E_{kin}. This, in turn, determines the velocity along the trajectory. The total time interval required for a run from q_{k0} to q_k need not be specified separately. For further discussion, see the book on tensors.

We wish to consider a stable system, with no particle running to infinity; such a system will be multiperiodic with no secular term. We thus *assume a multiperiodic* solution, where all quantities (E_{kin}, for instance) can be expanded in multiple Fourier series of type (IX.10):

$$E_{kin} = \sum_m C e^{2\pi i t (m \cdot v) + 2\pi i (m \cdot w_0)} \tag{IX.31}$$

The integration (IX.30) yields[1]

$$S = 2 \sum \frac{C_m}{2\pi i (m \cdot v)} e^{2\pi i t (m \cdot v) + 2\pi i (m \cdot w_0)} \tag{IX.32}$$

The question now is *what happens when the denominator* $(m \cdot v)$ *is zero* (complete *degeneracy*) or even simply very small (as small as desired, approximate degeneracy)?

It is at once obvious that such conditions are critical and may mean divergence of the multiple Fourier series, hence the impossibility of building up the function S. We must here consider two distinct problems: separated or nonseparable variables.

When *variables can be separated*, there is absolutely no coupling between a q_k variable and another q_1 one. There exist *no cross-terms* either in the kinetic or in the potential energy. As a result, there must be no cross-terms in the Fourier expansion (IX.31) and no troublesome terms in equation (IX.32):

$$S = S_1(q_1) + S_2(q_2) + \cdots S_k(q_k) + \cdots S_n(q_k) + \sum_k n_k J_k \quad (n \text{ integers}) \tag{IX.33}$$

The transformation function is a sum of separate functions of each variable, but a function $S_k(q_k)$ is only defined modulo J_k for the simple reason that we may use, from the initial q_{k0} to the final q_k position, an arbitrary trajectory making m_k loops (each of frequency v_k). Each S_k can be separately expanded in a single Fourier series

$$S = \sum_k \left\langle \sum_{m_k} \sum_{m_k} C e^{2\pi i m_k v_k t + 2\pi i m_k w_{0k}} + n_k J_k \right\rangle \tag{IX.34}$$

where we recognize at first sight the absence of any term in

$$(m \cdot v)t = (\sum m_k v_k)t$$

---

[1] Let us specify clearly the difference between Eq. (IX.24) and Eq. (IX.32). Equation (IX.24) contains the "unperturbed" frequencies v_0 corresponding to the H_0 Hamiltonian. In the other equation (IX.32) the formula works with the final v frequencies corresponding to the full problem ruled by the complete Hamiltonian H, including the so-called perturbation. Either one of these formulas can be used and may be more convenient for discussion.

The problem may be nonlinear in each separate variable, but cross-terms are not allowed. As noted in Section 3, the total energy is a function of the J_k action variables [Eq. (IX.9)], which are themselves analytic.

If the variables cannot be separated, the situation is completely different. Poincaré's theorem proves that in the most general case the J_k quantities *cannot be analytic*, and our formula (IX.32) shows that *the S function diverges*. The Hamilton–Jacobi procedure collapses. This is what happens if we make no special assumption about the Hamiltonian.

Many authors, including M. Born and L. Brillouin in previous papers, overlooked the nonanalyticity of the J's in the general case, and assumed that one could still write a formula of type (IX.9), giving the energy as a function of the J's. It would, however, be completely meaningless to express a well-behaved expression, the energy, as a function of nonanalytic quantities, the J's. The whole method simply does not work in the most general problems, when no restriction is used to limit the values of the C_m coefficients.

10. Sketch of a Discussion of the Possibilities of Convergence for Nonseparated Variables

We found that the Hamilton–Jacobi method works perfectly for separated variables, but does not work, in general, for nonseparated variables: where is the exact limit between these two extremes? We may find problems of "approximate separation" where a solution is still possible, provided certain conditions are fulfilled.

Let us consider again a perturbation problem, with a Hamiltonian:

$$H = H_0 + \lambda H_1 \tag{IX.14}$$

where H_0 is the unperturbed system with separation of variables and H_1 perturbation with coupling terms between variables.

We may discuss this problem according to the perturbation method of Sections 5 and 6. We look for an expansion of our function S [see Eq. (IX.20)]

$$S = S_0 + \lambda S_1 + \lambda^2 S_2 \ldots \tag{IX.20}$$

where S_0 corresponds to separation and is represented by Eq. (IX.33), while $S_1, S_2 \ldots$ contain the whole series of terms as in Eq. (IX.21):

$$S_1 = \sum_m \frac{A_m}{2\pi i(m \cdot \nu_0)} e^{2\pi i (m \cdot w)} \tag{IX.21}$$

where ν_0 represents the unperturbed frequencies. We discussed such formulas at the end of Section 6, and we followed Born's distinction between (A) nondegenerate problems, where no $(m \cdot \nu_0) = 0$ relation can be found, and (B) degenerate problems, with some $(m \cdot \nu_0) = 0$ relations.

This distinction, however, looks rather artificial.

In a nondegenerate situation (A), we still have an infinite number of infinitely small $(m \cdot \nu_0)$ denominators and the corresponding numerators A_m must be extremely small if divergence is to be avoided. In a degenerate case (B), as soon as one denominator $(m \cdot \nu_0)$ is zero, there is an infinite number of other $(pm \cdot \nu_0)$ zero denominators (p an integer), and all the corresponding numerators must be zero. The distinction is really superficial.

The actual problem is concerned with the convergence of the series of coefficients $A_m/(m \cdot \nu_0)$ which should be discussed. The multiple Fourier series for $S_1, S_2 \ldots$ are all of the same type (IX.21) where m stands for the set of indices $m_1, m_2, \ldots, m_N$. These series converge only when the series of the coefficients $A_m/(m \cdot \nu_0)$ are absolutely convergent. If this be the case, the S function can be constructed, and the Hamilton–Jacobi method works correctly.

If the absolute convergence of the multiple series of the coefficients $A_m/(m \cdot \nu_0)$ cannot be proven, the multiple Fourier series for S diverges, the Hamilton–Jacobi method collapses and we are in the "general situation" described by Poincaré. In order to achieve convergence, it is obviously necessary that the A_m coefficient become zero as $(m \cdot \nu_0)^\alpha$ with an exponent $\alpha \geq 1$; it is also required that the A_m's themselves decrease fast enough for very large values of the $m_1, m_2 \ldots m_N$ indices. When such conditions are fulfilled, the Hamilton–Jacobi method can be used, and it extends beyond the case of separated variables. These examples may be called problems of approximate separation.

11. DISCUSSION OF A SIMPLE EXAMPLE WITH TWO VARIABLES; DEGENERACY MEANS INSTABILITY OR RESONANCE

Degeneracy occurs when one frequency is zero, or when a condition of commensurability exists between the original frequencies. If the zero frequency corresponds to one of the variables of the motion, then it usually means a situation of instability. Such is the case for a rigid pendulum oscillating with very large amplitudes and reaching the top with zero velocity, whence it may fall back either to the right or to the left. The condition of commensurability will be shown to correspond to *resonance* between two or more degrees of freedom.

Let us sketch the problem for a system with two variables, hence two unperturbed frequencies ν_{01} and ν_{02}. Figure 20 visualizes the general situation: in a plane, we use the $m_1\nu_{01}$ as abscissae and $m_2\nu_{02}$ as ordinates (m_1, m_2 integers). Degeneracy holds when one of the points of the rectangular lattice happens to fall upon the second diagonal DOD'.

$$(m \cdot \nu) = m_1\nu_{01} + m_2\nu_{02} = 0 \qquad \text{or} \qquad m_1\nu_{01} = -m_2\nu_{02} \qquad \text{(IX.35)}$$

On our diagram, this is almost the case for $m_1 = 4, m_2 = -5$. The numerators $A_{m_1 m_2}$ must be zero along the diagonal line DOD'. When the variables are exactly separated, the $A_{m_1 m_2}$ are different from zero only along the axis 1 and the axis 2, and remain zero everywhere else in the plane.

Approximate separation holds when the $A_{m_1 m_2}$ become zero along DOD' and decrease suitably at large distance.

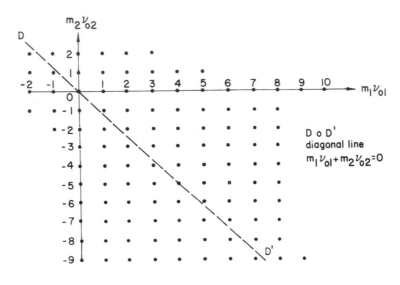

FIG. 20.

Let us now consider the case of *divergence* and try to understand the physical meaning of the difficulty encountered. Condition (IX.35) means internal *resonance*: the m_1 harmonic of ν_{01} coincides with the m_2 harmonic of ν_{02}. This certainly must cause trouble, since it is well known that resonance leads to infinite terms when no damping is available.

In many problems with no damping terms (neither positive nor negative), it happens that coupling between two oscillations at resonance may destroy resonance and give rise to two distinct frequencies. This is, in a different language, the well-known result that any perturbation (coupling) applied upon a degenerate system (having internal resonance) will lift the degeneracy (destroy resonance).

When two periods $m_1 \nu_{01}$ and $-m_2 \nu_{02}$ happen to be almost equal in the unperturbed problem, there is no complication so long as the variables remain completely separated and uncoupled. But when we introduce inter-coupling through the λH_1 perturbation term [Eq. (IX.14)], we must be prepared for the possibility of a large finite energy transfer from ν_{01} to ν_{02} through internal resonance, even when the λH_1 coupling is extremely small. This is another way of explaining the difficulties discussed in Section 5. It would be interesting to discuss carefully what happens in a variety of cases of internal resonance, for different types of nonlinear problems with nonlinear coupling, and to discover progressively the type of interactions that can take place.

Let us now refer again to the note in section 9. We find difficulties when some resonance appears between the *unperturbed frequencies* $v_{01}, v_{02}, \ldots, v_{0N}$, but we do not know whether any such resonance can take place between the final frequencies $v_1, v_2, \ldots, v_N$, defined in Section 9. There are indications that exact resonance between the final (actual) frequencies v may not possibly occur, and this again is a point requiring careful discussion.

12. Some General Conclusions. Determinism versus Statistical Mechanics

We discussed problems of classical mechanics, assuming that the model under consideration was stable, with no part of it escaping to infinity. The motion was considered as represented by a multiperiodic solution. In such a problem, the Hamilton–Jacobi method can be used only when the expansion of the transformation function S is convergent. This condition is automatically satisfied for separated variables, and may be satisfied for "almost separated" variables. In the general case the S expansion diverges, and Poincaré's great theorem definitely proves that the whole method is worthless.

The problem can be examined from two different angles, giving two distinct and even opposing points of view: the pure mathematical aspect first, and the viewpoint of a physicist, second.

The preceding considerations were based on a purely *mathematical* discussion. It was assumed that a trajectory could be defined by "given" initial conditions, the values of the coordinates and momenta at time $t = 0$ being exactly known, with no possible error. It was also assumed that the laws of motion were absolutely correct, with no deviation whatsoever. These two assumptions led to the consideration of a single trajectory considered as an infinitely thin mathematical curve. The periods of the multiperiodic motion were supposed to be exactly known, and questions were raised about their commensurability. The answers to the problem were distinguished as "general" or "degenerate", depending upon whether the periods were incommensurable or commensurable.

To all these definitions, the *physicist* raises some very serious objections. His position is the following:

A. Initial conditions are not "given"; they must be measured and observed. This means that the coordinates x_i and momenta p_i are known within errors Δx_i and Δp_i.

B. The laws of motion are no better known. They result from experiments, and they summarize a large number of previous observations. The simple laws selected for this representation must be considered only as a first approximation. The famous laws of Newton's mechanics are no exception, and the proof of this statement has been repeatedly given: these laws had to be amended and corrected in many instances, for relativity, for quantum theory, etc.

From these premises it is easy to draw some obvious conclusions, which were already stated by E. Borel (1914), M. Born (1953, 1959) and Brillouin (1957, 1958, 1959), and which were sketched briefly at the end of Section 1 of this paper:

A. The notion of an *irrational* number is nonphysical. It is impossible to prove that a physical quantity is rational or irrational.

B. The notion of *commensurability* is nonphysical, when the quantities to be compared are known only to within some experimental errors.

C. It is impossible to study the properties of a single (mathematical) trajectory. The physicist knows only *bundles of trajectories*, corresponding to slightly different initial conditions. E. Borel, for instance, computed that a displacement of 1 cm, on a mass of 1 gram, located somewhere in a not too distant star (say, Sirius) would change the gravitational field on the earth by a fraction 10^{-100}. The present author went further and proved that any information obtained from an experiment must be paid for by a corresponding increase of entropy in the measuring device: infinite accuracy would cost an infinite amount of entropy increase and require infinite energy! This is absolutely unthinkable.

D. Let us simplify the problem, and assume that the laws of mechanics are rigorous, while experimental errors appear only in the determination of initial conditions. In the bundle of trajectories defined by these conditions, some may be "nondegenerate" while others may "degenerate." The bundle may soon explode, be divided into a variety of smaller bundles forging ahead in different directions. This is the case for a model corresponding to the kinetic theory of gases. Borel computes that errors of 10^{-100} on initial conditions will enable one to predict molecular collisions for a split second and no more. It is not only "very difficult," but actually impossible to predict exactly the future behavior of such a model. The present considerations lead directly to Boltzmann's statistical mechanics and the so-called "ergodic" theorem.

The problem is of such importance that it requires a few more words of explanation. Recalling the results of Section 10, we must distinguish among three different possibilities:

1. *Separated variables.* We use the variables w_k and J_k introduced in Section 3. The J_k retain constant values through the bundle and are defined within errors ΔJ_k that depend only upon the errors made about initial conditions. These ΔJ_k remain constant in the course of time. The problem was discussed in great detail in Chapter VIII. The angle variables w_k exhibit very different behavior. The error Δw_k increases steadily in the course of time, and

after a while it may become larger than 2π, which means that we know no longer what this angle may be.

In such problems, the J_k are well-behaved functions, but the angles w_k are not. Of course, predictions about the w_k values may be good for a certain period of time, right at the start; or even (if initial conditions are very exactly defined) the predictions may be correct for a rather long interval of time (as is the case in astronomical problems), but in the long run the uncertainty over the phase angles must always become dominant.

2. *Almost separated variables.* Similar conclusions may hold but for the fact that the $J_k w_k$ variables now result from a contact transformation based on the function S instead of a point transformation.

3. *General case* (Poincaré). No S function can be constructed, and the total energy is the only well-behaved function in a system of coordinates where the center of mass is at rest.

For separated or almost separated variables, we almost obtain *determinism* at the beginning, but after a certain time interval the angles w_k are no longer observable, although the momenta J_k are still well-behaved integrals of the motion.

In the general case, the total energy is the only quantity about which predictions can be made.

E. We may choose another simplified alternative and assume initial conditions to be rigorously "given" but fix our attention on the fact that the laws of mechanics are only a first approximation. These classical laws correspond to an "unperturbed" Hamilton function H_0, which may be completed by some unknown small perturbation λH_1. What is the role played by this perturbation? This is practically the question answered by Poincaré in the famous theorem quoted in Sections 2 and 7. In the general case, the total energy comes out as the only well-behaved analytic solution of the initial conditions. It appears that the Poincaré theorem contains the justification of Boltzmann's statistical mechanics, which should apply when (and only when) the total energy of the system actually remains the only well-behaved first integral.

F. All these approximations must be carefully weighed and discussed. For some problems (kinetic theory of matter) they make predictions almost impossible. For other types of problems (astronomy) the situation is not so hopeless. The fundamental question to be discussed is the *stability of the solution* for small changes in the initial conditions or in the Hamiltonian. This question has been too often overlooked.

G. Classical mechanics assumes that it is reasonable to speak of two trajectories that may be infinitely close together. If then there is a finite difference in a certain quantity between these trajectories, it means a real discontinuity and a nonanalytic function.

Wave mechanics, applied to a stable problem, gives proper ψ functions, defined by quantum numbers. These functions (or the corresponding semi-classical trajectories) can never be infinitely close; they remain at finite intervals, and all quantities normally exhibit finite differences.

The transition from wave mechanics to classical mechanics is obtained by the *B.W.K. method*, but it should be emphasized that this method has *been discussed only for problems with separated variables*. The transition from wave mechanics to classical mechanics for nonseparated variables is an open question.

We shall examine a variety of examples in the next chapter.

REFERENCES

Borel, E. (1914). "Introduction géométrique à quelques théories physiques," p. 94. Gauthier-Villars, Paris.

Born, M. (1925). Vorlesungen über Atommechanik, collection "Struktur der Materie," Vol. 2. Springer, Berlin. English translation: M. Born, "The Mechanics of the Atom." Bell, London, 1927.

Born, M. (1953). Physical reality. *Phil. Quart.* **3**, 139.

Born, M. (1955). Continuity, determinism and reality. *Kgl. Danske Videnkab. Selskab. Mat.-fys. Medd.* **30**, No. 2.

Born, M. (1959). *J. Phys.* **20**, 43.

Brillouin, L. (1938). "Les tenseurs en mécanique et en élasticité." see Chapter VIII, paragraphs 12–16, especially p. 171. Masson, Paris. These definitions were systematically used by L. Boltzmann in his lectures on mechanics.

Brillouin, L. (1957). Mathematics, physics, and information. *Inform. & Control* **1**, 1.

Brillouin, L. (1958). *Ann. Phys.* **3**, 243.

Brillouin, L. (1959). *Nature* **183**, 501.

Brillouin, L. (1964). "Tensors in Mechanics and Elasticity." Academic Press, New York.

Poincaré, H. (1892–1899). "Méthodes nouvelles de la mécanique céleste," 3 vols. Gauthier-Villars, Paris. Reprinted by Dover, New York.

Poincaré, H. (1902). "La Science et l'Hypothèse." Flammarion, Paris. English translations: The Foundations of Science. Containing: Science and Hypothesis, The Value of Science, Science and Method. Science Press, New York, 1929.

Chapter X

EXAMPLES OF UNCERTAINTY IN CLASSICAL MECHANICS[1]

1. INTRODUCTION

Poincaré's famous theorem was published in Volume I, Chapter V of his "Méthodes nouvelles de la mécanique céleste" (1892); its fundamental result is:

In the most general conservative problem, the canonical equations of classical mechanics do not admit any analytical and uniform integral beside the energy integral.

The great importance of this theorem is well known; it was discussed in Chapter IX, where it was shown that this condition resulted in discontinuities in the solutions obtained by the Hamilton–Jacobi method; it may be explained by the following statement:

For a given mechanical problem with energy conservation and no dissipation, one may find a few variables that can be separated away from the system. When this has been done, one is left with the hard core of nonseparable variables. This is where the Poincaré theorem applies, and specifies that the total energy is the only expression represented by a well-behaved mathematical function. Many other quantities may appear as "constants" of a certain given motion, but they cannot be expressed as analytical and uniform integrals. This means that any kind of modifications in the definition of the problem may provoke an abrupt and sudden change of the "constants." This discontinuity may be the result of a very small change in any parameter in the mechanical equations, or, also, in any small change in the initial conditions. Max Born quoted this discussion of the present author in a very interesting

[1] Sections 1–9 are revised from a paper by the author first published in *Inform. & Control* **5**, 223–245 (1962).

paper published in the Jubilee Volume offered to W. Heisenberg on his 60th birthday (Born, 1961).

Poincaré's original theorem applies to a *conservative* mechanical system (no dissipation, no feedback, no internal source of energy). If any parameter entering the equations is varied, then one might think of power series expansions, with respect to this parameter, that should represent the perturbed motion, but, according to Poincaré, these power series will not be analytic and continuous, and uniform convergence will not obtain. Hence the possibility of discontinuities or sudden changes.

This situation, of course, corresponds to practical instability. It is physically impossible to measure accurately all the parameters defining the system. The mathematician speaks of a parameter with "a certain given value" and admits that this value is strictly defined, without any possible error. The physicist knows that nothing can be measured accurately, that our theories, even the best ones, are only acceptable within certain limits and that we have to take into account errors of measurement in all possible applications. Under such conditions, the above-mentioned instability corresponds to a situation where the theory is unable to yield a well-defined solution.

This general point of view was emphasized in the author's books (Brillouin, 1959, 1962) and many recent papers (Brillouin, 1957, 1959, 1960).

2. THE HAMILTON–JACOBI METHOD

Let us recall a simple example and consider the manner in which Born uses it (Born, 1925) in atomic problems. We take a conservative mechanical system, without friction and without energy supply. The total energy is the sum of kinetic and potential energies:

$$E_{\text{tot}} = E_{\text{kin}} + E_{\text{pot}} \tag{X.1}$$

Let us call $x_1 \cdots, x_K \cdots, x_N$ the variables, and $p_1 \cdots, p_K \cdots, p_N$ the corresponding momenta of the system under consideration; these quantities, moreover, may depend on a certain number of parameters $\alpha_1, \alpha_2 \cdots, \alpha_n$ capable of varying from one case to the other. The initial conditions $x_{10} \cdots$, x_{N0}, and $p_{10} \cdots, p_{N0}$ are not rigorously "given" but we have been able to *determine* them experimentally with errors $\Delta x_{10} \cdots, \Delta x_{N0}$, and $\Delta p_{10} \cdots, \Delta p_{N0}$.

The Hamilton–Jacobi method seeks a transformation enabling us to replace the variables x_K, p_K by some new variables W_K, J_K (Delaunay) which satisfy the following conditions:

$$E_{\text{tot}} = F(J_1 \cdots J_K \cdots J_N) \tag{X.2}$$

The total energy is a function only of the new momenta $J_1 \cdots J_N$ which remain constant while the angular variables W_K have linear dependence on time:

$$W_K = \nu_K t + W_{0K} \qquad \nu_K = \frac{\partial F}{\partial J_K} \qquad (X.3)$$

On the whole, we obtain a multiperiodic motion, with partial periods ν_K. We refer the reader to the classical book by Born (1925) for all additional explanations. This multiperiodic motion seems to present a character of stability, as Poincaré pointed out. Each coordinate x_K is defined by a relation:

$$x_K = f_K(W_1 \cdots W_N) \qquad (X.4)$$

with a periodic function f_K (period, 2π) with respect to all W_K's. No physical coordinate x_K can increase till infinity, which is a character of stability.

Note, however, that the *quantities J_K, W_{0K} are not continuous functions* of the x_{0K}, p_{0K} nor of the α_m. The smallest variation of the parameter α_m or the smallest change in the initial values may bring on discontinuous variations of the J_K, W_{0K} and lead to a solution completely different from the previous one. And this is incontestably, a special type of instability, imposed by Poincaré's theorem, though incompletely studied and not fully understood in all its consequences.

Let us go back to Eq. (X.2) and emphasize the paradox: the total energy is always a continuous function of the parameters of the movement. But the Hamilton–Jacobi method defines this energy as a function F of the quantities J_K which are not continuous. This looks like a strange challenge: it is necessary that the function F present discontinuities which exactly compensate those of the J's. What is then the meaning of the derivatives $\partial F/\partial J_K$ which yield frequencies ν_K? It seems very mysterious. It is not exaggerated to say that the Hamilton–Jacobi method has some very definite shortcomings. Its very elegant formalism is spoiled by Poincaré's discontinuities.

3. CONDITIONS OF DISCONTINUITY AND CASES OF RESONANCE

These general remarks leave an unfortunate impression, and some examples are necessary to understand the exact meaning of the preceding statements.

First of all, let us specify *the conditions when* discontinuities may occur. Born's discussion (1925), Poincaré's theorem, and their comparison (Brillouin, 1960) clearly show that disontinuities may appear whenever a compound frequency is zero:

$$\nu_n = \sum_K n_K \nu_K = 0 \qquad (X.5)$$

where the n_K's are positive or negative integers. Some authors believed it possible to overcome the difficulty by saying that everything is all right as long as the frequencies are incommensurable, but this is not acceptable in a real physical problem where all quantities (v_K's included) are defined only within certain possible errors Δv_K. Moreover, it is sufficient that at certain compound frequencies v_n be very small, without being identically naught, for divergent series to appear. These series may be semiconvergent and seem perfectly sufficient to yield approximate solutions, but they cannot supply an exact mathematical solution.

Let us note, for more precision, that condition (X.5) contains cases of *internal resonance*. Let us consider a system depending upon two angular variables W_1, W_2 and therefore two frequencies v_1, v_2. Condition (X.5) is thus written:

$$n_1 v_1 = -n_2 v_2 \tag{X.6}$$

Let us take $n_2 = -n'_2$ with n'_2 positive, and we obtain a condition of internal resonance between harmonic n_1 of v_1 and harmonic n'_2 of v_2. The internal resonance gives a typical case of instability through discontinuity.

4. ONE DEGREE OF FREEDOM AND A SINGLE FREQUENCY EQUAL TO ZERO

The first example to consider corresponds to a problem with a single variable and a single frequency v. This frequency may depend upon initial conditions and also upon a certain number of parameters in the definition of the problem. We are thus led to consider the meaning of the condition:

$$v = 0 \tag{X.7}$$

Let us immediately take an example: the *circular pendulum*.

A rigid pendulum is sustained by an axis around which it can turn. When slightly touched, the pendulum oscillates on both sides of the vertical. Violently thrown, it will turn indefinitely. The discontinuity occurs when the pendulum has been thrown with just enough energy to reach the top and stay in the unstable vertical position. Will it then fall to the left or will it fall to the right? In one case, it will start a series of long oscillations; in the other case, it will turn indefinitely (while slowing almost to zero each time it reaches the top). The top position yields an infinite period and zero frequency.

$$v = 0 \qquad \tau = \infty$$

This is a typical example of condition (X.7).

We discussed a variety of one-dimensional problems in Chapter VIII, where we found it useful to draw some figures, representing the momentum p as a function of the variable θ. In the present problem, the potential energy is represented by the curve of Fig. 21, where V_1 represents the potential energy for the vertical pendulum.

One type of motion yields small oscillations (A) about the origin 0 (Fig. 22). The second type of motion (B) corresponds to a continuous increase of θ. The limiting curve is represented by motions where p is going to zero at $\theta = \pi$, 3π, 5π and this motion has zero frequency.

Instead of the pendulum we may consider a ball running through a system of periodic hills and valleys represented by Fig. 21 (change θ to x and replace

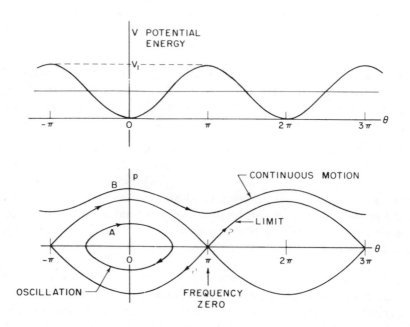

FIGS. 21 & 22.

π by the distance from hill to valley). The motions of Fig. 22 correspond to oscillations within one valley (case A) or long distance motion through valleys and up above the hills (case B). The limiting case is that of a ball rolling up the hill and standing still in this unstable position.

Figure 21 corresponds to an infinite succession of equidistant valleys and hills. We may equally well have only a finite number of valleys, with potential walls on both sides. Figure 23 shows two valleys with high potentials left and right. The motion A yields oscillations about the bottom of the valley on the left, while A', with the same energy, oscillates in the valley on the right side. For energy just equal to V_1 (saddlepoint) the p, x trajectory has the ∞ shape; the velocity (or p) is zero at point 0, which means $\tau = \infty$ and $\nu = 0$. For higher energies (B) the diagram runs around both points I and II; it oscillates within the two valleys, from the left wall to the right wall. There is discontinuity at the ∞ shaped curve, of energy V_1.

In most physical problems, the potential energy drops to zero at infinite distance, when interaction between particles is naught. This yields a potential

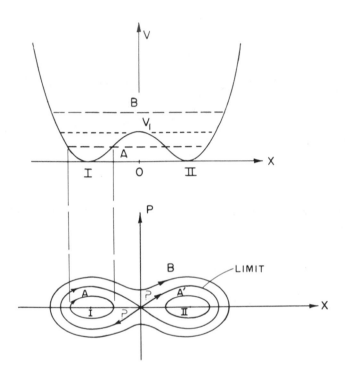

FIGS 23. & 24.

curve of the type drawn on Fig. 25. The point at infinity is a maximum of potential, and zero energy corresponds to a Poincaré discontinuity (Fig. 26). The saddlepoint 0 of Fig. 24 is here removed to infinite distance.

Each point, in the p, x diagrams, where the trajectories intersect (point π on Fig. 22, or 0 on Fig. 24 or the point at infinity on Fig. 26) is a branching point where the trajectory may go one way or another (Fig. 27). Let us assume, as we did previously, in Chapter VIII, that initial conditions are not exactly given but have been experimentally measured with some degree of uncertainty. Initial data are contained in a small area α, which moves to the branching point and splits there in two parts, one part β following one trajectory and the other part β' going the opposite way. This is the physical meaning of Poincaré's discontinuities.

We may also understand from these figures, how it happens that the total energy E is a continuous function of the initial data, while the integral J is not continuous. We emphasized this curious result at the end of Section II.

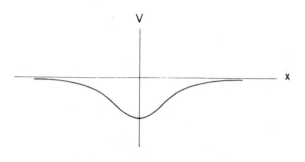

FIG. 25.

Let us consider Fig. 24 and assume the motion to start from the left part of the x axis:

$$x < x_1 \qquad p = 0$$

The first trajectories are of type A and the integral

$$J = \int_0 p \, dx \tag{X.8}$$

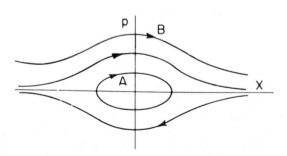

FIG. 26.

measures the area enclosed in the A trajectory. There is obviously a sudden change of this area when we pass from trajectory A to trajectory B, and this does not yield any sudden change in energy E.

These new results complete and modify the description given in previous chapters and give a much greater importance to uncertainties in the definition of the motion. The *Poincaré discontinuities* correspond to conditions where *prediction is actually* impossible and determinism cannot exist.

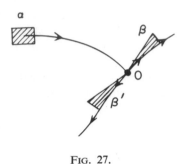

FIG. 27.

5. Motions in Space

Problems in two and three dimensions lead to many generalizations of the previous results. To be realistic we must consider actual physical problems where interactions between particles tend to zero at infinite distance, and the potential energy at infinity can be taken as zero. Any trajectory reaching infinity with zero velocity is thus a Poincaré limit trajectory, and we have an infinite variety of such trajectories. Speaking of astronomy and trajectories about an attractive center (say, the sun), we note the existence of periodic motions (Kepler's ellipses); the larger they become, the lower their frequency; in the limit, the ellipse reaching infinity is a *parabola*, of *frequency zero*, and marks the border between ellipses and hyperbolas. This is a typical example of instability, to be kept in mind.

In addition to these infinite trajectories, we may have all sorts of other complications when we consider many attractive centers instead of just one. Some saddlepoints of the potential energy will appear, each of them giving rise to trajectories of zero frequency, which represent the limit between different types of orbits; some orbits circle about one center, others move around two or more centers of attraction. We must emphasize again the sharp distinction between systems with (or without) *separation of variables*. This point had already been clearly stated in Chapter IX, where the question was discussed in Sections 9–12, especially at the end of Section 12.

When variables can be *separated*, each one of them behaves like a system with a single variable, and the discussion of Section 4 applies. When variables *cannot be separated*, the so-called general solution with Hamilton–Jacobi methods appears to be very artificial, and we must candidly admit that we cannot solve such problems exactly (this author does not know of any such problem ever solved!) and that our series expansions for successive approximations are not too reliable. Poincaré's theorem definitely proves that these series expansions do not converge. At best they can be semiconvergent. Assuming this to be the case, we can compute approximate solutions for a limited time interval, but a strictly rigorous solution cannot be obtained. We may compute, within a reasonable approximation, what will happen to the solar system for one century, but we do not know the outcome for an infinite time interval.

There is *no strict determinism* in classical mechanics, especially when we keep in mind the most important fact: the system is not "given" but "*measured with limited accuracy*" over past periods of time. There is always some experimental uncertainty in initial conditions and this uncertainty grows progressively in future times.

We may return to a problem in two dimensions and the condition (X.6) for internal resonance:

$$n_1 v_1 = n_2' v_2 \tag{X.6}$$

Figure 28 visualizes the situation and corresponds to the well-known

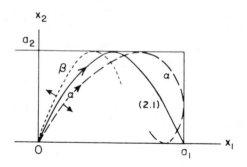

Fig. 28.

"Lissajoux curves." Coordinate x_1 oscillates from 0 to a_1, and back (period τ_1) while x_2 varies from 0 to a_2 with a period τ_2. The case $n_1 = 2$, $n_2 = 1$ of Eq. (X.6) means

$$\tau_1 = 2\tau_2 \qquad 2v_1 = v_2$$

When τ_1 is smaller, one gets the α curve; if on the contrary τ_1 is larger, curve β is obtained. In one case, the curve moves away from the original curve, to the right. In the other case, it moves to the left. Many similar problems may be found in atomic physics, with "rosette motions." One perturbation provokes a precession to the right; while an opposite perturbation yields precession to the left.

Furthermore, a condition (X.6) cannot be considered too strictly, as a mathematician would do. Frequencies v_1 and v_2 are experimentally determined with limited accuracy; their ratio also is known to a limited number of digits. Hence it can always be approximated by a decimal fraction. A mathematician would say that the ratio must be irrational, in order to prevent degeneracy (X.6), but an experimental measurement cannot distinguish irrational from rational.

Let us think of a TV spot scanning the screen. When the distance between lines is smaller than the diameter of the spot, it becomes impossible to say whether a relation (X.6) is satisfied or not!

6. COUPLED OSCILLATORS

We explained in Section 3 [Eqs. (X.5) and (X.6)] that we had to beware of internal resonances. This can be best observed in systems of coupled oscillators. Let us first summarize briefly the well-known problem of two *coupled linear oscillators*. We assume a potential energy V and a kinetic energy E_k:

$$V = \tfrac{1}{2}a_{11}x_1^2 + a_{12}x_1x_2 + \tfrac{1}{2}a_{22}x_2^2$$
$$E_k = \tfrac{1}{2}m_{11}\dot{x}_1^2 + m_{12}\dot{x}_1\dot{x}_2 + \tfrac{1}{2}m_{22}\dot{x}_2^2 \tag{X.9}$$

where x_1 and x_2 are the variables of both oscillators, while a_{12} and m_{12} represent *static and kinetic coupling* terms.

Equations of motion are easily obtained:

$$\left(m_{11}\frac{\partial^2}{\partial t^2} + a_{11}\right)x_1 + \left(m_{12}\frac{\partial^2}{\partial t^2} + a_{12}\right)x_2 = 0$$
$$\left(m_{12}\frac{\partial^2}{\partial t^2} + a_{12}\right)x_1 + \left(m_{22}\frac{\partial^2}{\partial t^2} + a_{22}\right)x_2 = 0 \tag{X.10}$$

We look for a "proper" vibration of frequency ω; hence we simply replace $\partial^2/\partial t^2$ by $-\omega^2$ and get

$$A_{11}x_1 + A_{12}x_2 = 0$$

with $\qquad A_{ik} = A_{ki} = -m_{ik}\omega^2 + a_{ik} \tag{X.11}$

$$A_{21}x_1 + A_{22}x_2 = 0$$

The linear Eqs. (X.11) have a solution when the determinant is zero.
$$0 = |A| = A_{11}A_{22} - A_{12}^2$$
$$= m_{11}m_{22}[(\Omega_{11}^2 - \omega^2)(\Omega_{22}^2 - \omega^2) - K^2(\Omega_{12}^2 - \omega^2)^2] \tag{X.12}$$

with

$$\Omega_{ik}^2 = \frac{a_{ik}}{m_{ik}} \quad\text{and}\quad K^2 = \frac{m_{12}^2}{m_{11}m_{22}}$$

Ω_{11} and Ω_{22} are the proper frequencies of uncoupled oscillators and K

represents the coupling coefficient. The vibrations in the coupled system are not localized in a single oscillator; on the contrary both oscillators are vibrating together

$$x_1 = X_1 \cos \omega t \qquad x_2 = X_2 \cos \omega t$$

$$-\frac{X_1}{X_2} = +\frac{A_{12}}{A_{11}} = +\frac{A_{22}}{A_{12}} \qquad (X.13)$$

Internal resonance occurs when Ω_{11} and Ω_{22} are almost equal. The net result is best seen on the graph of Fig. 29. The frequency ω in the coupled system is

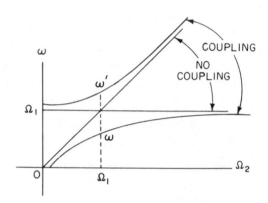

FIG. 29.

plotted as a function of Ω_{22} (proper frequency 2 without coupling). When coupling K is zero, the plot consists of the horizontal line ($\omega = \Omega_{11}$) and the line at 45° ($\omega = \Omega_{22}$). Both lines intersect at

$$\omega = \Omega_{11} = \Omega_{22}$$

With coupling ($K \neq 0$) the frequency is given by Eq. (X.12) and is represented by two hyperbolic-looking curves which no longer intersect. When Ω_{22} is equal to Ω_{11}, the frequency ω in Eq. (X.12) is given by

$$\Omega_{11} = \Omega_{22} \qquad \omega^2 = \Omega_{11}^2 \pm K(\Omega_{12}^2 - \omega^2) \qquad (X.14)$$

hence

$$\omega^2 = \frac{\Omega_{11}^2 \pm K\Omega_{12}^2}{1 \pm K}$$

These formulas yield two frequencies ω and ω', one above, and the other one below, Ω_{11}. For one of these frequencies, oscillations are in phase (X_1 and X_2 positive) while opposition of phases obtains for the other frequency ($X_1 > 0$, $X_2 < 0$). If the system is excited without special care, both ω and

ω' values will be excited together, and the motion will exhibit *beats* (or modulation) at frequency $\omega - \omega'$. This is schematically explained in Fig. 30. Experimental textbooks describe these beats under the nickname of "sympathetic pendulums."

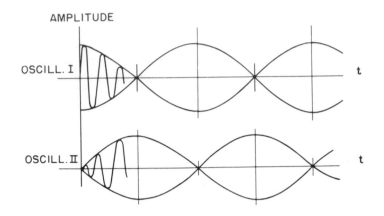

FIG. 30.

We may now sketch what happens when *one of the oscillators*, the first one, for instance, is *nonlinear*. This means replacing Eq. (X.10) by

$$\left(m_{11}\frac{\partial^2}{\partial t^2} + a_{11}\right)x_1 + \left(m_{12}\frac{\partial^2}{\partial t^2} + a_{12}\right)x_2 = \gamma\varphi(x_1)$$

$$\left(m_{12}\frac{\partial^2}{\partial t^2} + a_{12}\right)x_1 + \left(m_{22}\frac{\partial^2}{\partial t^2} + a_{22}\right)x_2 = 0$$

(X.15)

where φ can be any function of x_1, and γ measures the amount of non-linearity. We shall not discuss the general problem, but we shall assume small coupling and very small nonlinearity.

$$K \text{ small} \qquad \gamma \text{ very small} \qquad \gamma^2 \text{ negligible} \qquad (X.15a)$$

The function φ can be expanded in power series

$$\varphi = \alpha_0 + \alpha_1 x_1 + \alpha_2 x_1^2 + \alpha_3 x_1^3 \cdots$$

If x_1 is $X_1 \cos \omega t$ then x_1^2 gives a term in $X_1^2 \cos 2\omega t$, x_1^3 yields a term in $X_1^3 \cos 3\omega t$. ... As an example, let us assume

$$\varphi = \alpha_0 + \alpha_2 x_1^2 \qquad (X.15b)$$

We may try the following system of successive approximations: For the zero order, we set $\gamma = 0$ and solve the system (X.10) as previously discussed. We select one of the two possible frequencies, say ω, and obtain

$$x_{10} = X_1 \cos \omega t \qquad x_{20} = X_2 \cos \omega t \qquad (X.16)$$

as in (X.13).

This is our zero-order approximation with *dominant frequency* ω. For the *first-order* approximation we use x_{10} in φ and assume a small γ coefficient

$$\varphi = \alpha_0 + \alpha_2 X_1^2 \cos^2 \omega t = \alpha_0 + \tfrac{1}{2}\alpha_2 X_1^2 + \tfrac{1}{2}\alpha_2 X_1^2 \cos 2\omega t \qquad (X.17)$$

This expression appears on the right-hand side of Eq. (X.15). The constant term $(\alpha_0 - \tfrac{1}{2}\alpha_2 X_1^2)$ is of no special interest, and the term in $2\omega t$ will excite vibrations of frequency 2ω in x_1 and x_2. We thus look for solutions x_{11} and x_{21} in this first order approximation

$$x_1 = x_{10} + x_{11} \qquad x_{11} = Y_1 \cos 2\omega t$$
$$x_2 = x_{20} + x_{21} \qquad x_{21} = Y_2 \cos 2\omega t \qquad (X.18)$$

and we have linear equations with right-hand term:

$$A_{11}(2\omega) Y_1 + A_{12}(2\omega) Y_2 = \tfrac{1}{2}\gamma\alpha_2 X_1^2$$
$$A_{21}(2\omega) Y_1 + A_{22}(2\omega) Y_2 = 0 \qquad (X.19)$$

When the determinant is not zero, with

$$A_{ik}(2\omega) = -4m_{ik}\omega^2 + a_{ik}$$
$$= m_{ik}[\Omega_{ik}^2 - 4\omega^2] \qquad (X.20)$$
$$|A_{ik}(2\omega)| \neq 0$$

this set of equations is easily solved

$$Y_1 = \frac{\tfrac{1}{2}\gamma\alpha_2 A_{22} X_1^2}{|A|} \qquad Y_2 = -\frac{\tfrac{1}{2}\gamma\alpha_2 A_{12} X_1^2}{|A|} \qquad (X.21)$$

We thus obtain small corrections $Y_1 Y_2$ of order γ to be used in Eqs. (X.18).

This situation however changes completely when the determinant is very small

$$|A(2\omega)| \approx 0 \qquad (X.22)$$

We already discussed the determinant $|A|$ in Eq. (X.12) and called ω, ω' its two roots. We may use either ω or ω' in the zero-order approximation in these two cases, and we have the following

$$\text{using } \omega \qquad |A(2\omega)| = 0 \qquad \text{giving } 2\omega = \omega'$$
$$\text{using } \omega' \qquad |A(2\omega')| = 0 \qquad \text{giving } 2\omega' = \omega \qquad (X.23)$$

These conditions represent internal resonances between one of the frequencies and the second harmonic of the other frequency. This anomaly corresponds exactly to the Poincaré condition (X.6). It requires a special treatment because Y_1 (or Y_2) may become of the same order of magnitude as X_1 (or X_2), and our assumption of a single dominant term is no longer acceptable.

This problem has been discussed more completely by Magiros (1960, 1961) who has been able to obtain solutions for these abnormal conditions. Discontinuities again result from the Poincaré condition in this example.

In all problems of vibration, it is a general result that *coupling between oscillators results in an increase of the frequency differences*. In other words, frequencies seem to be repelling each other.

7. Some Examples in Astronomy

A. The Case of Collisions

This example was discussed by Poincaré himself (Poincaré, 1892), and leads to obvious discontinuities: a particle A may pass a particle B without collision, and follow its own way normally; or A may strike B and be deviated. The two motions are completely different, and the smallest change in the initial conditions is sufficient to pass from one trajectory to another.

B. A Satellite Near the Earth

The earth is not a sphere but has the shape of a flat ellipsoid. The trajectory of an artificial satellite has been computed by a method of successive approximations by Brouwer (1959) who found an unstable motion for the inclination of 63°. A special case, permitting a separation of the variables was discovered by Vinti (1959, 1961) who obtained no unstable trajectory except for the ones passing by the poles. There is a lack of convergence in the development computed by Brouwer when the inclination reaches 63° and this anomaly corresponds to an internal resonance [similar to Eq. (X.6)] between the frequencies of the zero-order approximation. This internal resonance is shifted to a different inclination in the first-order approximation, and is again shifted in the following approximations; it would certainly reach the polar trajectory in the final stage.

In other words, this is a case where a relation

$$n_1 \nu_{10} = n_2' \nu_{20} \qquad \text{(X.24)}$$

where ν_{10}, ν_{20} are zero approximation frequencies, is progressively shifted to

$$n_1 \nu_1 = n_2' \nu_2$$

where $\nu_1 \nu_2$ are actual final frequencies.

This change was predicted in Chapter IX. This type of problem was discussed in general terms in Section 9, and it was emphasized that the actual Poincaré condition should contain the frequencies ν_k of the final problem, while the discussion based on a set of successive approximations seemed (by mistake) to contain the original unperturbed frequencies ν_{k0}. It is obvious, at first sight, that any condition based on the arbitrary model selected for the zero-order approximation should be modified after approximations of higher order have been introduced.

In all cases, what we had foreseen actually occurs: a very small modification in the initial conditions or in the structure of the system is enough to produce a finite change of the trajectories. Such is the kind of discontinuity which corresponds to the absence of uniform convergence demonstrated by Poincaré.

These anomalies make it impossible to predict exactly the behavior of the system for any distant time, and lead directly to statistical mechanics. We may repeat here an example given by Borel, and already quoted in Chapter IX.

A displacement of 1 cm for a mass of 1 gm located on the star Sirius results in a variation of the earth's field of gravitation greater than 10^{-100}. This seems negligible at first sight, but such a perturbation gives us the possibility of computing the motion of the molecules of a gas for a duration of about 1 millionth of a second; prediction for any longer time becomes impossible. The example chosen by Borel supplies him with a wonderful justification for the statistical methods of Boltzmann, but at the same time it raises the problem of cases of instability, less obvious but no less real. Those are the examples which Poincaré's conditions clearly specify.

8. PROBLEMS OF APPLIED MECHANICS

All the problems discussed in the preceding sections corresponded to the usual situation in classical mechanics: no friction, no viscosity, no damping of any sort. This applies to celestial mechanics, and this assumption is pre-supposed in Poincaré's papers. The conditions of instability discovered by Poincaré have, however, a far-reaching validity, and extend to problems of applied mechanics, where all sorts of damping terms (positive or negative) may be essential. We will not discuss such problems in detail; they can be found in the many books and papers on mechanical vibrations. Let us only sketch some of the mechanical examples and show how internal resonances yield instability.

Coupled oscillators without resistances were discussed in Section 6; but actual oscillators are always damped. Continuous oscillations can be generated if the first oscillator contains a *negative resistance* (sustaining the motion) while the second oscillator is damped by a positive resistance. This problem can be discussed in general terms and leads to results sketched in Figs. 31 and 32. Figure 31 corresponds to small coupling; the hyperbolic curves obtain for zero resistance and the heavy curve represents the frequency of sustained oscillations. The ratio of intensities in both oscillators is plotted on the lower curve. If the frequency of oscillations kept a constant value Ω_1, we would obtain a correct resonance curve (dotted line), but the reaction of the second oscillator on the first one provokes a displacement of the frequency ω which seems to be repelled away from Ω_2. As a result, the actual resonance curve looks sharper than normal.

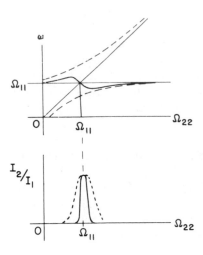

FIG. 31.

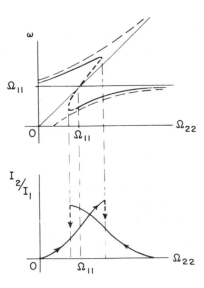

FIG. 32.

Figure 32 corresponds to strong coupling; the frequency ω is now represented by a Z-shaped curve, with the medium part unstable. It extends quite a distance along both branches of the original (no resistance) curve. The resonance curve, in this case, splits into two different branches, with sudden transitions from the upper branches to the lower branches. There is no more continuity but sharp discontinuities between different types of motion (Brillouin and Armagnat, 1923; Cruft Electronic Staff, 1947; see next section). Many examples of this kind are found in electronically sustained circuits. Let us quote a mechanical problem: a watch hanging on a nail. The first (sustained) oscillator is the watch's balance-wheel; the second (damped) oscillator is the pendulum consisting of the watch on the nail. When both are nearly in resonance, the watch goes fast or slow, depending on circumstances.

9. NEGATIVE RESISTANCES IN OSCILLATORS

It may be useful to sketch briefly the meaning of *negative resistance*. A great many electric, electronic, and semiconductor devices yield some rather complicated characteristics, where the current I, plotted as a function of voltage V, may show a negative resistance R along some branches of the curve:

$$\frac{1}{R} = \frac{dI}{dV} \qquad R = -R' \quad R' > 0 \tag{X.25}$$

Such a device, if conveniently connected (or coupled) to a circuit, may yield a negative resistance in the circuit, and compensate the normal positive resistance, thus making it possible to obtain sustained oscillations. All negative resistance devices are strongly nonlinear, and the average negative resistance R depends upon the amplitude of oscillations. Altogether these devices are able to yield (depending upon the amplitude) a negative resistance

$$R_m' \leq R' \leq R_M' \qquad R = -R' \tag{X.26}$$

comprised between two limits R_m' and R_M'. This general statement suffices for an elementary discussion.

Let us assume a negative resistance in the first oscillator of Eq. (X.10), and a normal positive resistance in the second oscillator. This means adding a term in $-R'\dot{x}_1$ in the first equation and a term $+r\dot{x}_2$ in the second. Let us also assume no potential coupling ($a_{12} = 0$, hence $\Omega_{12} = 0$). We investigate the possibility of sustained oscillations in $e^{i\omega t}$, and we obtain both Eqs. (X.11) with:

$$A_{11} = m_{11}(\Omega_{11}^2 - i\rho_1\omega - \omega^2) \qquad m_{11}\rho_1 = R'$$

$$A_{12} = -m_{12}\omega^2 \tag{X.27}$$

$$A_{22} = m_{22}(\Omega_{22}^2 + i\rho_2\omega - \omega^2) \qquad m_{22}\rho_2 = r$$

where ρ_2 has a given value, while ρ_1 can take any value between the limits resulting from (X.26). Condition (X.12) now reads

$$(\Omega_{11}^2 - i\rho_1\omega - \omega^2)(\Omega_{22}^2 + i\rho_2\omega - \omega^2) - K^2\omega^4 = 0 \qquad (X.28)$$

We must split real and imaginary terms

$$-\rho_1(\Omega_{22}^2 - \omega^2) + \rho_2(\Omega_{11}^2 - \omega^2) = 0$$
$$(\Omega_{11}^2 - \omega^2)(\Omega_{22}^2 - \omega^2) + \rho_1\rho_2\omega^2 - K^2\omega^4 = 0 \qquad (X.29)$$

The first condition gives the value of ρ_1 for which sustained oscillations may occur

$$\rho_1 = \rho_2 \frac{\Omega_{11}^2 - \omega^2}{\Omega_{22}^2 - \omega^2} \qquad (X.30)$$

This value, substituted in the second equation, yields an equation of third degree in ω^2 (after multiplying by $\Omega_{22}^2 - \omega^2$)

$$(\Omega_{11}^2 - \omega^2)(\Omega_{22}^2 - \omega^2)^2 + \rho_2^2(\Omega_{11}^2 - \omega^2)\omega^2 - K^2\omega^4(\Omega_{22}^2 - \omega^2) = 0 \qquad (X.31)$$

The ratio of amplitudes (X.13) X_1/X_2 is complex. The amplitude of oscillations depends upon nonlinear terms in the negative resistance characteristics, and this nonlinearity will provoke some harmonics in the oscillation.

The discussion is based on the following remarks:

At *exact resonance* ($\Omega_{11} = \Omega_{22}$) there is always a solution

$$\Omega_{11}^2 = \Omega_{22}^2 = \omega^2$$

Far from resonance the solution is close to Ω_{11} (or, more explicitly, to the solution of a system with zero resistance)

$$\Omega_{22} \gg \Omega_{11} \qquad \text{or} \qquad \Omega_{22} \ll \Omega_{11} \qquad \omega \approx \Omega_{11}$$

This is obvious from (X.30) which gives a small ρ_1 value and makes the $\rho_1\rho_2\omega^2$ term in the second Eq. (X.29) negligible if ρ_2 is small. These remarks lead directly to the two situations sketched in Figs. 31 and 32.

10. WHEEL SHIMMY IN CARS; WING FLUTTER IN AIRPLANES

A different situation may be found in many electrical and mechanical problems; it corresponds to structures with coupled oscillators characterized by *active coupling*. In the model of the preceding section there was energy fed into one oscillator by the negative resistance, but the coupling mechanism was passive. This can be seen in the fact that we could start from conservative equations (X.9) and (X.10), and obtain our equations (X.11) with symmetrical coupling terms

$$A_{12} = A_{21} \qquad (X.32)$$

The problems which we now want to discuss are characterized by a coupling that may feed energy into the system of coupled oscillators. This results in nonsymmetrical equations

$$A_{12} \neq A_{21} \qquad (X.33)$$

Well-known examples are wheel shimmy in cars and wing flutter in airplanes. The vibrations of wheels in a car are coupled through friction on the ground and this reaction from ground friction may feed energy into the vibrations of the wheels. As for airplane wing flutter, it is due to the coupling between two distinct vibrations of wings, and this coupling is modified by the wind, that may bring energy into the system.

The problem of wing flutter is very clearly investigated by Karman and Biot (1940) where the reader finds an excellent discussion on pages 220–228. The character of active coupling is emphasized at the bottom of p. 224 where it is shown to result directly from the dissymmetry (X.33).

Let us sketch a simplified mathematical model where Eqs. (X.11) are replaced by

$$A_{11}x_1 + A_{12}x_2 = 0$$
$$A_{21}x_1 + A_{22}x_2 = 0 \qquad (X.34)$$

$$A_{11} = m_{11}(\Omega_{11}^2 - \omega^2)$$
$$A_{22} = m_{22}(\Omega_{22}^2 - \omega^2) \qquad (X.35)$$
$$A_{12}A_{21} = -\alpha^2$$

For wing flutter, the coefficients A_{12} and A_{21} have opposite signs, and we do not have any terms in Ω_{12} or Ω_{21}. Equations are usually nonlinear, and α^2 may depend upon amplitude of oscillations.

Both Eqs. (X.34) are compatible only when the determinant $|A|$ is zero, hence

$$(\Omega_{11}^2 - \omega^2)(\Omega_{22}^2 - \omega^2) + \chi^2 = 0$$
$$\text{with } \chi^2 = \frac{\alpha^2}{m_{11}m_{22}} \qquad (X.36)$$

This equation differs from Eq. (X.12) since it contains a positive term $+\chi^2$ instead of the negative term $-K^2(\Omega_{12}^2 - \omega^2)^2$. The corresponding plot exhibits two hyperbolic branches as shown in Fig. 33, but these branches are different from those in Fig. 29 on account of $+\chi^2$ instead of $-K^2(\Omega_{12}^2 - \omega^2)^2$. Between Ω' and Ω'' the solution shows oscillations with exponential growth. As a matter of fact, the amplitude of the oscillations will increase until the intervention of nonlinear terms that will dissipate energy, thus exactly compensating for the fed-in energy. There will thus be sustained oscillations (with variable amplitudes) all along the dotted curve, between Ω' and Ω''.

The detail of the curves evidently depends upon mechanical details in the dissymmetrical coupling system and the actual problem is much more complicated; the simple example which we just outlined, however, contains the essential points.

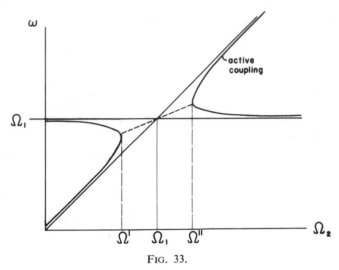

FIG. 33.

Let us note the main differences with the problems discussed in Section 6.

A. Nonconservative systems, connected to exterior energy sources.

B. Dissymmetrical coupling.

C. The frequencies come together and merge in the maintained-oscillations region, whereas, in Section 6, the frequencies repelled each other.

11. TRANSITION FROM CLASSICAL MECHANICS TO WAVE MECHANICS

All the problems exhibiting internal resonances and leading to Poincaré's discontinuities exhibit, in wave mechanics, very specific anomalies. In the usual problems, the passage from classical mechanics to wave mechanics can be easily discussed with the help of the B.W.K. (Brillouin, Wentzel, Kramers) method. We will not linger on this scheme of successive approximations, which can be found in all classical textbooks, especially in Kemble's (1937). When Poincaré's conditions are taken into account, the discussion becomes more involved.

Let us consider, for example, a particle moving in a field with periodical potential, as in Fig. 21. Wave mechanics leads to a Mathieu Equation, and the solution is very different when the energy is inferior or superior to the limit V_1. This problem was discussed on various occasions and we will only refer the reader to the book by Brillouin (1953). Figure 34 illustrated the situation. When the energies are inferior to V_1 the motion consists in oscillations within the valleys; this yields very narrow energy bands E_1', E_2'. When the energies come closer to V_1, the bands widen and become very wide above V_1. Classical mechanics yielded a discontinuity, with completely different motions for energies below or above V_1. Wave mechanics suppresses the discontinuity and replaces it with a progressive transition.

The problem of Fig. 23 leads to similar remarks. Physicists, in their jargon express the fact by saying that the oscillations in valleys I and II are "coupled through a tunnel-effect across hill V_1," so that the passage from one valley to the other is possible, even for energies slightly inferior to V_1. In any case, Poincaré's conditions, for a classical case, lead to very particular situations in wave mechanics.

We will not stress here the role of internal resonances in wave mechanics: it is well known that they raise problems of degeneracy.

12. Wave Scattering

We mentioned in Section 7 that collision problems evolved from Poincaré's conditions, and had, from the beginning, been given as examples by Poincaré himself. In wave mechanics, the *collision* problem becomes a *scattering* problem: a plane wave is supposed to fall upon an obstacle; the problem is to calculate the distribution of the radiation scattered and the scattering cross section. A good number of such examples can be found in optics or in acoustics. Let us take a problem in optics and let us consider a spherical obstacle with a perfectly reflecting surface. It is generally admitted that geometrical optics (which corresponds to classical mechanics) obtains as a limiting case of wave optics when the frequency becomes infinite and the wavelength tends to zero. In fact, things are not that simple, and the passage at the limit hits unforeseen obstacles, as we are going to explain.

Essentially, here is the problem: a plane light wave (wavelength, λ) is falling upon a sphere of radius a, which may be a dielectric or exhibit some conductivity. Compute the scattered wave and scattering cross section. The problem has been discussed by G. Mie and P. Debye around 1905 (Stratton, 1941). Let us consider a limiting case, when the sphere is made of an ideal metal of very large radius $a \gg \lambda$. The computed cross section for scattering is $2\pi a^2$, *twice as large as the geometric cross section* πa^2! However, in this limiting case, geometrical optics should apply; yet the latter predicts an amount πa^2 of light scattered in all directions, plus the shadow. How can these results be reconciled?

The situation is still more obscure when the same theory is used (P. Debye) to compute the radiation pressure on the sphere. This pressure corresponds to a cross section πa^2 in the limit of large metallic spheres!

In a former paper (Brillouin, 1949), the whole theory was carefully rebuilt and it was proven that, for the light scattered at large angles, both wave theory and geometrical optics agreed very well. The difficulty was about the *shadow*. The perfect shadow of geometrical optics is an unrealistic idealization. Wave optics replaces this picture with a complicated system of beams of light scattered at very small angles, interfering together and with the incident light. This mathematical description yields, physically, a circular

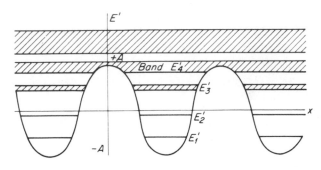

FIG. 34.

shadow accompanied by a complicated system of diffraction fringes, which are specially noticeable near the border of the shadow. These fringes build up a sort of penumbra around the shadow and they spread out progressively when distance increases (see Fig. 35). At a distance of the order of

$$R \approx \frac{3a^2}{\lambda} \qquad a \gg \lambda \qquad (X.37)$$

or larger, the penumbra extends practically all over the previous shadow and starts spreading farther and farther while the shadow fades away and cannot be clearly seen anymore. A careful selection of asymptotic formulas to be

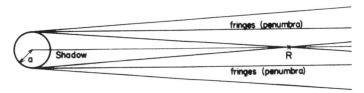

FIG. 35.

used for this discussion leads to the simple result that the amount of light scattered at *large angles* corresponds to a cross section πa^2, while the amount scattered at *very small angles* yields *another* πa^2. The total scattering cross section is actually the sum, $2\pi a^2$, but the second part is deflected by very small angles and does not contribute to radiation pressure; hence the πa^2 found by Debye in that second problem.

Experiments were made by Sinclair and La Mer with small spheres of radius $a = 15$ microns and light $\lambda = 0.5$ micron. Such conditions yield

$$R = 1350 \text{ microns, or } 1.35 \text{ mm}$$

Experiments proved that the light scattered decreased from 2 to 1 when observations were made at a large distance (18 feet) or very close to the glass plate supporting the spheres. This was a perfect check of the theory.

The conclusion is that the *true scattering cross section* is $2\pi a^2$! *Yes, but* how far do we have to go to be able to observe it? We must make observations at a distance far beyond the R value. The following table gives some orders of magnitude:

Let us take a wavelength of $0.3\ \mu$ (that is 3×10^{-5} cm) and let us compare the lengths of a and R

				0.1	10
$a\ \{$ km					
cm	10^{-2}	1	10^2	10^4	10^6
$R\ \{$ cm	10	10^5	10^9	10^{13}	10^{17}
km		1	10,000	10^8	10^{12}

For a sphere of 0.1 mm we obtain $R = 10$ cm; therefore, we are able to observe the geometrical shadow very close to the sphere or a wide fringed penumbra from a distance of a few meters. The experiment checks with the predictions. If we give the sphere a radius $a = 1$ meter, the distance R reaches 10,000 km, and experiments made on earth can only show the geometrical optics, with slight fringes around the shadow. If we study the shadow of the moon, we have to go to distances of hundreds of light years to find the limit R. The moon's radius being

$$a \approx 1,600 \text{ km} = 1.6 \times 10^8 \text{ cm}$$

$$\text{distance from the earth:} \quad d \approx 360,000 \text{ km} = 3.6 \times 10^{10} \text{ cm}$$

$$\text{critical distance for } \lambda = 0.5 \text{ microns} = 5 \times 10^{-5} \text{ cm}$$

$$R \approx 3\frac{a^2}{\lambda} = 3\frac{(1.6)^2}{5} 10^{21} \text{ cm}$$

$$R \approx \frac{3}{2} 10^{21} \text{ cm} = 1.5 \times 10^{16} \text{ km}$$

On the earth $(d \ll R)$, we can only observe the geometrical shadow and the geometrical scattered light. The *true scattering cross section* would require the observer to go to a fantastic distance, much larger than R which amounts approximately to 12 centuries of light speed!

Let us be frank: the true scattering cross section is impossible to observe under such conditions.

Furthermore, the general situation is the same for any kind of wave:

electromagnetic, elastic, ψ waves of L. de Broglie, for all sorts of particles, etc.; it is also very similar for any shape of the scattering body. Moreover, this must be considered a very typical instance where *wave mechanics* (or optics) *does not converge smoothly toward geometrical mechanics* (or optics). Both theories rejoin with a fight, resulting from a change in fundamental definitions and a change in conditions of observation.

Few scientists seem to *realize the importance of this very general problem.*

The transition *geometry → wave geometry* is therefore made progressively, but according to a quite unforeseen mechanism. The rigorous, *efficient cross section* is effectively given, *in all cases*, by the formula $2\pi a^2$ and remains equal *to the double of the geometrical cross-section. However*, in order to observe this value, theoretically incontestable, we have to go to an infinite distance, much greater than R and absolutely unreachable in practice!

Collision phenomena, in wave mechanics, therefore raise very critical problems.

13. Conclusion

A physicist and a mathematician do reason along different lines. The mathematician builds a theory upon a set of axioms and pursues his construction work to the most extreme limits. A physicist chooses a theory which supplies him with an acceptable *model* and allows him to represent empirical facts in a certain field, and according to certain *orders of magnitude*. Any theory is subject to these limitations. It is valid as long as it checks with experiments; pursued further, it might lead to absurdities.

Rational mechanics, it was said, is completely deterministic. One easily forgot to add that this determinism demands that the absolutely accurate measurement of the given data be possible. As soon as inevitable *errors in measurements* are taken into account, determinism collapses. This weakness is particularly serious for all cases of instability corresponding to Poincaré's conditions, and discussed in this chapter.

REFERENCES

Born, M. (1925). "Vorlesungen über Atommechanik." Springer, Berlin.

Born, M. (1961). Bemerkungen zur statistischen Deutung der Quantenmechanik. In the Jubilee Volume "Werner Heisenberg und die Physik unserer Zeit," p. 103. Vieweg, Braunschweig.

Brillouin, L., and Armagnat, H. (1923). "Les Mesures en haute fréquence," Chapter I, p. 12. Chiron, Paris.

Brillouin, L. (1949). The scattering cross section of spheres for electromagnetic waves. *J. Appl. Phys.* **20**, 1110.

Brillouin, L. (1953). "Wave Propagation in Periodic Structures," 2nd ed., 255 pp. Dover, New York.

Brillouin, L. (1957). Mathematics, physics and information (an Editorial). *Inform. and Control* **1**, 1–5.

Brillouin, L. (1959a). Inevitable experimental errors, determinism and information theory. *Inform. and Control* **2**, 45–63.

Brillouin, L. (1959b). "Vie, Matière et Observation," Chapters V and VI. Albin Michel, Paris.

Brillouin, L. (1960). Poincaré and the shortcomings of the Hamilton–Jacobi method for classical or quantized mechanics. *Arch. Rational Mech. Anal.* **5**, No. 1, 76–94.

Brillouin, L. (1962). "Science and Information Theory," 2nd ed. Academic Press, New York.

Brouwer, D. (1959). Solution of the problem of artificial satellite theory without drag. *Astron. J.* **64**, 378–397; Comments on general theories of planetary orbits, orbit theory. *Proc. Symposium Appl. Math., New York* **9**, 152–166.

Cruft Electronic Staff. (1947). "Electronic Circuits and Tubes," pp. 472–477. McGraw-Hill, New York.

Karman, T., and Biot, M. (1940). "Mathematical Methods in Engineering," p. 223. McGraw-Hill, New York.

Kemble, E. C. (1937). "Fundamental Principles of Quantum Mechanics." McGraw-Hill, New York. Reprinted by Dover, New York, 1958.

Magiros, D. (1959). On a problem of non-linear mechanics. *Inform. and Control* **2**, 297–309.

Magiros, D. (1960). A method for defining principal modes of non-linear systems utilizing infinite determinants. *Proc. Natl. Acad. Sci. U.S.* 1608–1611.

Magiros, D. (1961). Method for defining principal modes of non-linear systems utilizing infinite determinants. *J. Math. Phys.* **2**, No. 6, 869–875.

Poincaré, H. (1892). "Méthodes nouvelles de la mécanique céleste," Vol. I, Chapters V and VIII. G. Villars, Paris & Dover Pub., New York.

Stratton, J. A. (1941). "Electromagnetic Theory." New York.

Vinti, J.-P. (1959). *J. Research Natl. Bur. Standards, Ser. B* **63**, 105–116.

Vinti, J.-P. (1961a). *J. Research Natl. Bur. Standards, Ser. B* **65**, 131–135.

Vinti, J.-P. (1961b). Theory of an accurate intermediary orbit for satellite astronomy. *J. Research Natl. Bur. Standards, Ser. B* **65**, 169–201.

Books published by
L. Brillouin

Masson & Cie, Paris
"Cours de physique théorique: Les tenseurs en mécanique et en élasticité." 1st edition, 1937;
    2nd edition, 1949, one volume, 370 pages.
"Notions élémentaires de mathématiques pour les sciences expérimentales." 1st edition,
    1935; 2nd edition, 1938; 3rd edition, 1947, one volume, 284 pages.
"Propagation des ondes dans les milieux périodiques" (with M. Parodi). 1956, one volume,
    347 pages.
"La Science et la théorie de l'Information." 1959, one volume, 325 pages.

Presses Universitaires, Paris
"La théorie des quanta et l'atome de Bohr." 1923, 1 volume, 181 pages (out of print).
"La théorie des quanta, I." (2nd edition.) L'atome de Bohr; la mécanique analytique et les
    quanta; les spectres de multiplets. 1931, one volume, 364 pages.
"La théorie des quanta, II." (2nd edition.) Les statistiques quantiques et leurs applications.
    1930, two volumes, 404 pages.

Gauthier-Villars, Paris
Influence de la température sur l'élasticité d'un solide. *Mémorial des Sciences Mathé-
matiques.* No. 99 (1940), 65 pages.
"Jubilé de M. M. Brillouin pour son 80ème anniversaire." 1935, one volume, 40 pages.
"Jubilé scientifique de M. M. Brillouin, allocutions." 1935, one volume, 40 pages.

Chiron, Paris
"Les mesures en haute fréquence" (with H. Armagnat). 1923, one volume, 200 pages (out
    of print).

Hermann, Paris
Actualités scientifiques et industrielles
    No. 15 Les statistiques quantiques et leur application aux électrons libres dans les
            métaux, 1930, 44 pages.
    No. 39 Notions de mécanique ondulatoire, les méthodes d'approximation. 1932,
            35 pages.
    No. 59 La diffraction de la lumière par les ultrasons. 1933, 32 pages.
    No. 71 La méthode de champ self-consistent. 1933, 47 pages.
    No. 88 Les électrons dans les métaux, du point de vue ondulatoire. 1934, 35 pages.
    No. 89 Conductibilité électrique et thermique des métauz. 1934, 75 pages.

No. 159 Les champs self-consistents de Hartree et de Fock. 1934, 37 pages.

No. 160 L'atome de Thomas-Fermi et la méthode du champ self-consistent. 1934. 46 pages.

No. 549 La structure des corps solides dans la physique moderne. 1937, 53 pages.

No. 718 La théorie de la diffraction de la lumière par les ultrasons, 1938, 67 pages.

Albin-Michel, Paris

"La vie, la matière et la théorie de l'Information." 1959, one volume, 246 pages.

Springer, Berlin

"Quantenstatistik" (Struktur der Materie, Volume XIII). 1931, one volume, 530 pages.

Russian Translations of "Quantum Statistics," 1931.

"Bohr's Atom," 1932. "Wave Propagation," 1959. "Information Theory," 1960.

Blackie & Son, London

"Selected Papers on Wave Mechanics" (with L. de Broglie). 1928, one volume, 150 pages.

McGraw-Hill, New York

"Wave Propagation in Periodic Structures." 1946, one volume, 247 pages.

Dover, New York

"Wave Propagation in Periodic Structures," 2nd edition, 1953, 255 pages.

Academic Press, New York

"Science and Information Theory." 1956, one volume, 320 pages; 2nd edition, 1962.

"Wave Propagation and Group Velocity." 1960, one volume, 154 pages.

"Tensors in Mechanics and Elasticity," 1964, one volume, 478 pages.

"Scientific Uncertainty, and Information," 1964, one volume, 175 pages.

Subject Index